CAT TALES

Endearing, Eccentric and
Extraordinary True Stories

CAT TALES

Endearing, Eccentric and Extraordinary True Stories

TOM QUINN

Quiller

Text © 2016 Tom Quinn
Illustrations © 2016 Nicola L Robinson

First published in the UK in 2016
by Quiller, an imprint of Quiller Publishing Ltd

British Library Cataloguing-in-Publication Data
A catalogue record for this book is available from the British Library

ISBN 978 1 84689 229 5

Illustrated by Nicola L Robinson

Design and typesetting by Paul Saunders

Ptinted in Malta

Quiller

An imprint of Quiller Publishing Ltd
Wykey House, Wykey, Shrewsbury, SY4 1JA
Tel: 01939 261616 Fax: 01939 261606
E-mail: info@quillerbooks.com
Website: www.quillerpublishing.com

CONTENTS

Never wear anything that panics the cat.

P.J. O'Rourke

Time spent with cats is never wasted.

Sigmund Freud

I am fond of pigs. Dogs look up to us.
Cats look down on us. Pigs treat us as equals.

Winston Churchill

The smallest feline is a masterpiece.

Leonardo Da Vinci

We're all mad here.

Cheshire Cat from *Alice's Adventures in Wonderland*

INTRODUCTION

CATS HAVE KEPT humans company for as long as, if not longer than, dogs. For the ancient Egyptians cats were sacred; the penalty for killing one was death. Their importance can perhaps best be judged by the fact that, like humans, cats after death were mummified in their tens of thousands.

After settled agriculture began perhaps ten thousand years ago, cats would have quickly realised that living close to humans was not such a bad idea. Humans could be relied on to litter their encampments with odd bits of discarded food. Perhaps in the beginning these cats were driven off, but soon those early agriculturalists would have realised that the cat could be an immensely useful ally in the battle against grain-eating pests, especially rats a͞ mice. Even today, with modern methods of pest co͞ most farms will still have a cat patrolling the barns as they patrolled those ancient human settlements.

The cat's importance in this respect can be seen in the extracts from medieval Welsh laws that appear in this book; extracts that record their value and the fines imposed for ill-treating them.

Carefully bred to produce various physical and temperamental characteristics, cats have also, of course, long been valued as pets, from the sleek Burmese and the long-haired Persian, to the highly vocal Siamese, or the giant Maine Coon and the bizarre hairless Devon Rex.

Cats arouse our passions. Many dislike them because they kill wild birds, whilst others cannot bear to be without them.

The writer Anthony Powell, author of *A Dance to the Music of Time*, was not overly sentimental about cats, but he kept them all his life and wrote movingly about one particular favourite in this extract from his journal:

> The Trelawney (cat) situation has now come to the worst. He is a little bag of bones, finding difficulty in eating, lifting his head with an effort, tho' will jump on my knee. It breaks one's heart. Only six months ago the vet commented that it was nice to see a cat of Trelawney's age looking so well. He is now within a month of his eleventh birthday. V and John took him in today to the vet to make an end of things. I felt ashamed that this unpleasant job fell on them. Dreadfully distressing . . . A ·ry, very sad day.

Samuel Johnson, the author of the first comprehensive dictionary of English, was devoted to his cat Hodge. He worried that his servant Francis Barber might resent the cat if he were asked to go out and buy its food, so Johnson went himself.

The French poet and writer Théophile Gautier, extracts of whose writings are included in this book, was fascinated by cats, as was the Ancient Roman poet, Tasso. Poets Christopher Smart, William Cowper, and Oliver Goldsmith wrote about their favourite pets, as did Algernon Swinburne and Lord Byron. Lord Byron was probably only partly joking when he said that his cat Beppo helped him to write many of his greatest poems.

But writers are often solitary types and it is perhaps therefore not surprising that the solitary cat should appeal.

More surprising is the enthusiasm of journalist and former director of the RSPB, Philip Brown. In his book *The Cat That Came in From the Cold*, Brown recounts his great love of cats and his extraordinary success in teaching them to accompany him on hunting forays into the countryside.

And there are other surprises – the scientist Sir Isaac Newton, for example, was devoted to his cat, and the Prophet Mohammad was prepared to cut the sleeve from his coat rather than disturb his beloved cat, Muezza.

The appeal of cats is, nonetheless, hard to pin down. Partly, of course, it is simply the fact that cats are affectionate and loyal; the cat's independent nature is also part of it, but something elusive remains which is why, in a sense, this book is an attempt to capture the real nature of that elusive appeal through the eyes of famous and not so famous writers. Here you will find cats of all kinds – from the intelligent to the bizarre, from the endearing to the downright eccentric.

I have trawled through the archives to discover long-forgotten cat gems from regional and national news-papers, from long-vanished magazines and newspapers, and from obscure out-of-print books from the past two centuries published both here and in America.

There is nothing scientific about the stories and mem-ories that make up *Cat Tales*, but they are all true stories and I hope that they will go some way towards illumi-nating, if not quite explaining, our obsession with one of the most fascinating of all human companions.

Chapter One

CARING CATS

Mourning Moggie

I WONDER IF your readers can throw any light on the matter of the expression of grief by animals. I had a favourite Angora cat, who died after a week of suffering, the result of an accident. During his illness, his mother, a fine old cat of the ordinary sort, was often with him; but she was not present at the time of his death. He died late in the evening, and was taken into the cellar, to await his burial the next day. When he was brought up, stiff and cold, in a box, his mother was taken to see him; she gave one look, uttered a shriek, and ran away.

On relating this circumstance to a lady friend, she told me that there was a pet cat in her family, who was very fond of this lady's mother. When the latter was in her last illness, the cat was continually with her, lying on the bed.

The lady died, and the cat was, of course, not again admitted to the room, though presenting herself again and again at the door. When the coffin was being carried downstairs, the cat happened to appear, and, on seeing it, uttered a shriek.

In both these cases, the sound made was entirely unlike those made by cats under any circumstances, unless it be the cry made when in sudden pain.

In the latter case, the most remarkable part remains to be told. The cat went to the funeral, and then disappeared for many days. But after that, she repeatedly attended funerals at the same cemetery, walking before the clergyman her master.

E.T., *Spectator,* 14 March 1883

Frog Friend

I HAVE AN instance of strange friendship to mention. The servants of a country-house – and I am sure that they were kind people – had enticed a frog from its hole by giving it food.

As winter drew on, Froggy every evening made its way to the kitchen hearth before a blazing fire, which it found much more comfortable than its own dark abode out in the yard. Another occupant of the hearth was a favourite old cat, which at first, I daresay, looked down on the odd little creature with some contempt, but was too well bred to disturb an invited guest.

At length, however, the two came to a mutual understanding; the kind heart of Pussy warming towards poor chilly little Froggy, whom she now invited to come and nestle under her cosy fur. From that time forward, as soon as Froggy came out of its hole, it hopped fearlessly towards the old cat, who constituted herself its protector, and would allow no one to disturb it.

Daphne Seymour, *Kin and Kind*, 1870

Hare Trigger

CATS EXHIBIT their affectionate nature in a variety of ways. If deprived of their kittens, they have a yearning for the care of some other young creatures, which they will gratify when possible.

A cat had been cruelly deprived of all her kittens. She was seen going about mewing disconsolately for her young ones. Her owner received about the same time a leveret, which he hoped to tame by feeding it with a spoon.

One morning, however, the leveret was missing, and as it could nowhere be discovered, it was supposed to have been carried off and killed by some strange cat or dog. A fortnight had elapsed, when, as the gentleman was seated in his garden, in the dusk of the evening, he observed his cat, with tail erect, trotting towards him, purring and calling in the way cats do to their kittens. Behind her came, gambolling merrily, and with perfect confidence, a little leveret, the very one, it was now seen, which had disappeared.

Pussy, deprived of her kittens, had carried it off and brought it up instead, bestowing on it the affection of her maternal heart.

Time and Tide, January 1876

Old and Young

THERE IS ABUNDANT evidence that cats, as well as dogs, are capable of sympathising with one another when in trouble, and offering unselfish assistance. One of the prettiest stories of an old cat's kindness to a little one is told by Mrs Fyvie Mayo.

'One winter evening,' she says, 'as I was returning home about seven o'clock, I saw a large dog run breathlessly out of my garden gate, followed at a few paces by two ladies.

'When they saw me turning to enter, they spoke to me, saying that the dog I had seen had chased a tiny kitten, which they had succeeded in rescuing, and to secure its safety had handed into my hall, to be kept there till the pursuer was well out of the way.

'Going into my house I found that the kitten had been deposited on the dining-room sofa, a forlorn little mite, spitting and cursing in fury and fright. Vainly I offered it milk, vainly I coaxed it. It would not allow me to touch it, and it would not cease, nor even pause in its agitation.

'Suddenly I saw my dear old black cat, Yakoo, enter the room. Now Yakoo was an elderly bachelor of very comfortable habits, accustomed to his own way, and whenever youthful strays of his race had entered his sphere, he had hitherto regarded his duty to them as strictly limited to sound discipline!

'I trembled to think what severity, determined, though not harsh, this little angry stranger was bringing down upon himself.

'Lo! Yakoo looked thoughtfully at the trembling, excited bundle of fur upon the sofa, and then sprang up beside it. He did not touch it. He sat down about three feet away, and began talking to it. I say "talking" advisedly, for he did not mew; he purred and crooned, and was almost articulate. Just as one could understand, when another, speaking in an unknown language, is trying to soothe and reassure a fretted, frightened baby, so I could understand Yakoo.

'I am sure he asked that kitten what was the fuss. I am

sure he gave my household a good character for kind-liness. I believe he praised the quantity and quality of the food, and told the kitten he was a little simpleton not to know when he was well off. I am sure I was right, for see the effect on the kitten.

'The "spittings" grew less vivacious, and ceased. The growls grew so faint they passed into nothing. There was a pause, a sweet silence. The kitten moved towards the milk saucer. Yakoo watched it drinking. Then, with a con-tented purr he jumped off the sofa and walked away; and the kitten curled itself up and went to sleep. It showed no more fury or fright.

'Next day it was got into a good home, and had a very happy life.'

Could anything be more human-like, and wise and kind, than the behaviour of that fine old Tom?

Jennie Chappell, *Animals Worth Knowing*, S.W. Partridge, 1910

Warm-hearted

You quote from Sir J. Lubbock's Walsall lecture, where he says that a certain wasp 'knows whether the egg will produce a male or female grub, and apportions the food accordingly'.

Is it an absurd suggestion that the size of the cell and the amount of food supplied may determine the sex of the grub, and that all that the mother does is instinctively to fill the cell, regardless and ignorant of all consequences?

The case of the honey-bee is somewhat analogous; for if not sex, at least mature development, depends on conditions of food and cell; the worker-grub, properly fed and celled, can, as is well known, become a queen.

I can parallel your example of animal sympathy. I had a cat who carried to an old bitch who had partly suckled him, dainties to tempt her appetite in her last illness. But his feelings were more enduring. After the poor old dog had died, the cat would not for some time go near myself or the gardener, though previously much attached to both; evidently he thought we were implicated in the removal of his foster-mother.

Frater, *Spectator*, 19 February 1887

Professor Blackie

I KNOW YOU HAVE a high opinion of the dog's character, but of the 'harmless, necessary cat' perhaps you may not think so well as he or she deserves. The following anecdote of my own 'Black Beauty', or 'Professor Blackie', as I often call him, may find a place in your generous paper.

A favourite Pomeranian dog was cruelly blinded by a carter's lash, and, while his owner tenderly bathed the inflamed eyes, Blackie, the sleek tomcat, always sat by with a kindly look of pity in his luminous green eye.

When Laddie, the blind dog, was called in at night, he often failed to find the door, or would strike his venerable head against the posts.

Blackie, having noted this difficulty, would jump off his warm cushion by the kitchen fire, trot out with a 'mew' into the dark night, and in a few minutes return with Laddie shoulder-to-shoulder, as it were, and the friends would then separate for the night.

Laddie, when younger, had quietly resented the attentions shown by his owner to a fascinating kitten, who used to frolic with his long, fringed tail; but he was too noble to show active dislike. When the kitten died and its owner bent over the stiffened form in grief, Laddie came gravely up and kissed it. He followed to the grave, and for many days was seen by his mistress to go up the garden and sit upon the sod.

Was this his way of showing remorse for his former coldness, or might it be an expression of sympathy for his bereaved owner?

Manchester Guardian, 20 August 1887

The Cat's Canary

A FRIEND TOLD ME she knew an old lady, still living, who possessed a cat and a canary, both of which she was very fond. They both inhabited the dining room, and so far were well accustomed to each other's society.

The lady was aghast one afternoon, on opening the door, to see the room full of feathers; the bird cage was empty. Where was the bird? Alas! The cat crouched beneath the bird cage stand, its guilt too evident. Condign punishment was administered with many exhortations. How much did the cat understand? She slunk away, not to appear for many days and nights.

When at last she did appear she laid at the feet of her mistress a fluffy little canary, quite unharmed. The lady picked it up; it spread its wings and preened its plumage. She recognised the bird; it was a favourite of a friend living a few doors off. The cat also knew that bird, and had hovered about all those days and nights, watching for an opportunity to catch it, an offering to bring, in kind, to make up for its earlier bad behaviour.

Beatrice Braithwaite-Batty, *Strange but True*, 1931

Dog Lover

A POSTMAN WHO delivered letters at my brother's country house was accompanied by a poor, half-starved looking little dog. He explained that it was not his dog, but he did not push it away, because sometimes bits were thrown to it; so it got a little food.

One morning my sister-in-law went to speak to the postman at the front door; the cook stood at the side door some little way off; our cat, which was a great pet, was by her side with its saucer, which was half-full of some dainty food. The cat had been ill, and the cook was feeding it up.

To the amazement of all the onlookers, the cat presently proceeded across the lawn and rubbed noses with the dog, which followed her when she turned, and went straight to the saucer, evidently invited by the cat to do so.

The cat looked on until the saucer was cleared. Then the dog went back to the postman, wagging its tail by way of thanks for the hospitality enjoyed.

Beatrice Braithwaite-Batty, *Strange but True*, 1931

Bird Walk

THE FOLLOWING instance shows a natural instinct for prey, even when sharpened by hunger, being overborne by the power of attachment.

Mr A.H. Schippang of Bethlehem, Pennsylvania, has a cat and a quail which are fast friends. The bird, which was first of all adopted because it had injured its wing, became so tame that it would not fly away when liberated. The cat, 'Woollie', and 'Fritz' eat and sleep together, and the cat likes to have the bird walk all over him.

On one occasion during the summer it happened that the family all went away and left the two pets alone overnight. They left orders to the milkman to fill the cat's dish in the yard with milk, but in the flurry of setting out, Woollie was accidentally shut up in the little room where Fritz has his abode and lives in freedom.

When the family came back late next night they were horrified to hear Woollie scratching to get out of this room, and feared that hunger would have driven the cat to attack poor Fritz.

But notwithstanding his fast of two days and a night, Woollie had not touched his tiny friend.

Jennie Chappell, *Animals Worth Knowing*, S.W. Partridge, 1910

Looking after the Elderly!

Mrs. Moulton tells the following remarkable cat story:

'My mother had a cat that lived to be twenty-five years old. He was faithful and fond, and a great pet in the family, of course.

'About two years before his death, a new kitten was added to the family. This kitten, named Jim, immediately conceived the greatest affection for old Jack, and as the old fellow's senses of sight and smell failed so that he could not go hunting himself, Jim used to do it for both.

'Every day he brought Jack mice and squirrels and other game as long as he lived. Then, too, he used to wash Jack, lapping him all over as a mother cat does her kitten. He did this, too, as long as he lived. The feebler old Jack grew the more Jim did for him, and when Jack finally died of old age, Jim was inconsolable.'

The Times, 16 July 1840

Helping a Friend

Two cats, not related to one another, were simultaneously missed from their homes a short time ago, and did not appear for several days. Ultimately, quite by accident, they were discovered together in a loft, the one made prisoner by its foot being caught in a trap, and the other sitting beside it.

Round about them on the floor were the remains of dead birds, mice, etc., which the sympathiser had evidently caught and brought to his unfortunate friend. So busy had he been providing for the prisoner and bearing him company, that he had not had time once to go home to report himself to his owners.

Jennie Chappell, *Animals Worth Knowing*, S.W. Partridge, 1910

Lord Bountiful

A CAT-LOVER has two tabbies that are fed scraps of meat given them in a small vase. Recently, when feeding, one got a bit of meat out with her paw, while the other failed to do so. The first, on seeing this, left her own morsel untouched while she went and fished up a second piece for her brother, then she went back to eat her own.

The mother of these cats was wont to catch mice and bring them to her mother when the latter grew too old and feeble to hunt for herself.

We personally knew a cat who loved to play my Lady – or rather, my Lord – Bountiful to poorer animals of his acquaintance. 'Don' was a large tabby that lived in St Paul's Road, Canonbury. He was very fat, and much indulged, and not, on the whole, particularly interesting. But his strong point was charity. He was never without a poor pensioner.

'Skin', (so named by Don's mistress because of his appearance) benefited by Don's bounty for the longest period of all. Don would invite him into the scullery, and see him eat the pieces which he was himself too dainty to touch. He also allowed him, on washing days, to lie by the copper fire. But no further inside the house would he ever allow Skin to penetrate.

Sometimes on a cold, wet night, when Don returned from his evening walk, he would pause on the threshold of his home, and look back, refusing, for a time, to enter, Then Skin's timid nose would presently be seen peeping in at the back door, and Don would not go upstairs to his own place on the dining-room hearthrug until he had seen Skin have something to eat.

When he brought him indoors in that way it was generally in bad weather, and always because he had something to give him. Skin obviously worshipped Don, and would run to meet him with every expression of delight, and, when permitted, would kiss him. Don, however, would not always allow such familiarity, and if ever he considered that Skin in his demonstrations of affection was making too free, he would give him a sound slap on the face to teach him to keep his distance.

Three different strays did Don at various times bring home and befriend in this way; so it was evident that benevolence, of a patronising kind, was a fixed habit of his life.

We once possessed another cat that on one occasion brought home a stray kitten in a thunderstorm, and complacently watched the stranger eating his own food. This was also the clever animal, unless our memory is confusing him with another pet tabby of our childhood, that learned to release himself from a scullery where he was kept at night, by lifting the latch of the outer door.

No one, of course, saw him do this, for we were all in bed, but morning after morning the door was found open and pussy escaped. We gather, however, from writers on cat-lore, that this trick of manipulating a thumb latch is fairly common, the proceeding being always the same. The cat springs upon and clings to the bowed handle below the thumbpiece, and pats the latter till the door, by the animal's own weight, comes open.

Cats, perhaps from their greater springing and clinging power, are much cleverer at this accomplishment than dogs. An investigator of the subject, who made public request for instances of animals having learned to unfasten latches, reports that he quickly heard of half-a-dozen cats who had learned the trick, but only one dog.

Cats have certainly proved themselves very resourceful in accomplishing their desires. They seem to be both more ingenious and more persevering than dogs.

Jennie Chappell, *Animals Worth Knowing*, S.W. Partridge, 1910

Grave Matters

I HAD A DEAR little dog, a Skye terrier, and some time after he came to my house a wandered cat was added to the establishment.

He was very kind to 'Bessie', as we called our new inmate, and watched over her with great care, never allowing her to go out by the front door, but pushing her gently in when she attempted it; but they had many a romp together in the back garden.

My dog died at the good old age of thirteen, and the cat mourned him like a human being, losing all her liveliness, and moping about the house.

About a year after the dog's death I desired the gardener to put turf over his grave, as the house was let, and I feared strangers might dig there. To do this he began to level the earth over the grave, and whenever the cat saw him digging there she got into a most excited state, frisking about in the wildest spirits, evidently expecting that her kind companion was to be restored to her.

Her disappointment when he never appeared was trying to witness and she has been a sadder and wiser cat ever since doing her duty faithfully by the mice but apparently expecting little pleasure in life.

L.S., *Spectator*, 17 August 1895

For the Birds

ANIMALS OF A very different character often form curious friendships. What do you think of the cat which of
her own accord became the protector of a pet canary,
instead of eating it up?

The cat and the bird belonged to the mother-in-law of
Mrs Lee, who has given us many delightful anecdotes of
animals. The canary was allowed to fly about the room
when the cat was shut out; but one day their mistress,
lifting her head from her work, saw that the cat had by
some means got in; and, to her amazement, there was
the canary perched fearlessly on the back of Pussy, who
seemed highly pleased with the confidence placed in her.

By the silent language with which animals communicate their ideas to each other, she had been able to make
the canary understand that she would not hurt it.

After this, the two were allowed to be constantly
together, to their mutual satisfaction. One morning,
however, as they were in the bedroom of their mistress,
what was her dismay to see the trustworthy cat, as she
had supposed her, after uttering a growl, seize the canary
in her mouth, and leap with her into the bed. There she
stood, her tail stiffened out, her hair bristling, and her eyes
glaring fiercely.

The fate of the poor canary appeared sealed; but
just then the lady caught sight of a strange cat creeping

cautiously through the open doorway. The intruder was quickly driven away, when faithful Puss deposited her feathered friend on the bed, in no way injured – she having thus seized it to save it from the fangs of the stranger.

Confidence begets confidence; but be very sure that the person on whom you bestow yours is worthy of it. If not, you will not be as fortunate as the canary was with its feline friend.

M.R. Williamson, *Tales of Our Animal Friends*, 1852

Bruno's Chum

A FRIEND IN Cheshire tells me that when their large dog, Bruno, was lying sick and feeble with old age, a small, yellow barn-door kitten was so moved with pity for him, that she tried to nurse and mother him, even attempting the, to her, herculean task of washing his huge, thick coat with her tiny tongue! It was a pretty but pathetic sight.

At night she would nestle close to his side and purr to him, by day she could scarcely be persuaded to leave him.

'I am sure,' said my informant, who watched the pair, 'that Bruno thoroughly understood that the little kitten was trying in her small way to make him well.'

Jennie Chappell, *Animals Worth Knowing*, S.W. Partridge, 1910

Thieving Feline

An Angora cat, which lived in a large establishment in France, had discovered that when a certain bell rang the cook always left the kitchen.

Numerous niceties were scattered about, some on the tables and dressers, others before the fire. Pussy crept towards them, and tasted them; they exactly suited her palate. When she heard the cook's step returning, off she ran to a corner and pretended to be sleeping soundly.

How she longed that the bell would ring again. At last she thought that she would try to ring it herself, and get cook out of the way; she could resist her longing for those sweet creams no longer. Off she crept, jumped up at the bell rope, and succeeded in sounding the bell. Away hurried cook to answer it. The coast was now clear, and Pussy revelled in the delicacies left unguarded – being out of the kitchen, or apparently asleep in her corner, before cook returned.

This trick continued to answer Pussy's object for some time, the cook wondering what had become of her tarts and creams, till a watch was wisely set to discover the thief, when the dishonest though sagacious cat was seen to pull the bell, and then, when cook went out, to steal into the kitchen and feast at her leisure.

London Gazette, June 1901

Something to Crow About

I HAD A CAT for many years that refused utterly ever to catch a bird or a mouse. At first I thought this little rogue has no intention of earning his keep so far as mice are concerned, but he was charming company and I would not have parted with him for anything.

One day at the bottom of the garden by our small stream I found Hercules the cat sitting by a crow – now you will think that this crow must have been dead or at least fighting with Hercules for its life. But no; the crow was injured certainly, but the cat was simply sitting along-side and giving the bird an occasional glance.

On a whim that I cannot now explain, I decided to try to nurse the crow back to health. This I did and a few months later the bird (which was rather bad tempered with me) was quite well again, although she would never be able to fly.

What is most remarkable about this tale is that from the day I began to tend to the crow, Hercules became fascinated. He stayed close to the crow whenever he could and when the crow was well again and hopping about the kitchen and the yard the cat would accompany him everywhere. Both crow and cat seemed delighted at his arrangement and it lasted until Hercules died.

H.M.C., letter to *The Times*, August 1900

Giveaway

THAT WE MUST attribute to cats the estimable virtue of benevolence, Mrs F gives me two anecdotes to prove.

A lady in the south of Ireland having lost a pet cat, and searched for it in vain, after four days was delighted to hear that it had returned. Hastening to welcome the truant with a wassail-bowl of warm milk in the kitchen, she observed another cat skulking with the timidity of an uninvited guest in an obscure corner.

The pet cat received the caresses of its mistress with its usual pleasure, but, though it circled round the bowl of milk with grateful purrings, it declined to drink, going up to the stranger instead, whom, with varied mewings, 'like man's own speech', it prevailed on to quit the shadowy background and approach the tempting food.

At length both came up to the bowl, when the thirsty stranger feasted to its full satisfaction, while the cat of the house stood by in evident satisfaction watching its guest; and not until it would take no more could the host be persuaded to wet its whiskers in the tempting beverage.

Pets and Other Animals, Williams and Booker, 1888

Kind Hearts

SOME CATS seem to learn to be amiable to all the pets about their home. I have seen a story of one that was like a mother to some young guinea pigs, though she had kittens of her own too. The kittens and the guinea pigs used to play about her together. And she was very kind to some pigeons and little bantams which her mistress kept. None of them were a bit afraid of her. Yet when this cat went into the garden, or into the fields and roads, she caught birds if she could, and ate them, and enjoyed them as much as any other cat would have done.

And what of the cat at Lymington that took compassion on a brood of deserted young chickens – poor motherless little things she seemed to see that they were; and evidently she pitied them. Instead of eating them, as most cats would, she took them under her protection; and though she had two kittens of her own, she encouraged them to come and nestle about her, and keep themselves warm, as her own kittens did.

Thus the kittens and the chickens were brought up to play together, and be good friends. Of course the man who had care of the animals had to see that they were fed, but the cat took care that they did not get lost; for the master himself once saw her go after a stray chicken and bring it back. But all cats, as we know, are not so benevolent.

The Clan of the Cats, Seeley, Jackson & Halliday, 1877

Chapter Two

CLEVER CATS

Crumbs!

DURING A recent severe winter, a friend was in the habit of throwing crumbs outside his bedroom window. The family have a fine black cat, which, seeing that the crumbs brought birds, would occasionally hide herself behind some shrubs, and when the birds came for their breakfast, would pounce upon them with varying success.

The crumbs had been laid out as usual one afternoon, but left untouched, and during the night a slight fall of snow occurred. On looking out next morning, my friend observed puss very busily engaged scratching away the snow. Curious to learn what she sought, he waited, and saw her take the crumbs up from the cleared space, and lay them one by one after another on the snow. After doing this, she retired behind the shrubs to wait further developments.

This remarkable story receives confirmation from a friend who witnessed the action of a cat, that, having for some time feasted on the birds that were attracted by scattered crumbs, took to scattering them herself when the practice was discontinued by her owners.

Jennie Chappell, *Animals Worth Knowing*, S.W. Partridge, 1910

Tibs the Traveller

A SHORT TIME AGO we lived upon the shores of the Lake Lupioma (Clear Lake), which is one of the most beautiful lakes in California, and there I had a little cat, named 'Tibs'.

There was no regular road to our house on the shore, but only a horse-trail through the bush, and Tibs had never passed this way in her life, and all communication was by means of boat and steamers. When we removed from our home we came away in a boat, and after landing two miles further down got directly into a waggon, and rode seven miles up into the forest, where we now live.

We left poor Tibey behind, knowing she could get her own living very well, and meaning by and by to have her brought to us. Between the place where we now live and the shores of the lake there are two or three small farms, and all around them is forest. But there are innumerable roads, stretching away in every direction. These roads are made by the ox-teams of the wood-choppers; they are very dark and lonely, leading up the mountain-top and into the thickest parts of the pine forest, and then suddenly ending.

If you follow one of these, it will lead you many miles away, and then you will come to a spot where some enormous trees have been cut down and been dragged away by the oxen, and all beyond is the dark wood again.

Of course, I was very unhappy about my little friend, but we were all so busy that nobody had time to go and look after her. And so five weeks passed away. One evening, as we were sitting down to supper under a beautiful tall pine tree, we heard a faint mewling, and looking, saw our faithful little cat springing across the stream. We took her into our laps and nursed her all the evening.

This is surely one of the most remarkable feats of navigation. It's not even as if she was returning to a place she knew well.

San Jose News, May 1890

Written Evidence

A LITERARY FRIEND of mine at Bath had been often vastly amused at the interest with which her cat appeared to view her proceedings at the writing table. The cat would sometimes jump up beside her, and lay his paw on her wrist. On one occasion, however, he leapt on the table in front of her, and watched her narrowly, and with such a preternaturally knowing glance in his bright eye, with his head held slightly on one side, that she was impelled to lay down her pen and look at him.

What was her surprise and delight to see him walk deliberately to the inkstand, take a pen in his mouth, and leaping to the floor, commence tracing characters with it on the carpet, fortunately for which, poor Timothy had forgotten the ink. Another day his mistress said to him in fun, 'Oh, Timothy, I have lost a button off my dress; I wish you would find it!'

The animal looked at her, walked out of the room, and returned in a few minutes with the missing button in his mouth! Alas! poor Timothy he has disappeared, and this is probably the only permanent record of his winn-ing ways.

C.W., letter to The Times, 6 April 1900

Automaton

I HOPE YOU will consider as worthy of record an habitual action on the part of our 'conscious automaton' of the cat species, which certainly exhibits a well-connected train of thought.

In this old house there is a staircase with a borrowed light, admitted at a considerable height from the ground, through a balustrade, beneath which there hangs a bell.

When our 'automaton' finds himself on this staircase – without practicable egress – the door being shut, he leans forward through the balustrade, and literally 'touches the bell'. Of course, this summons always results in his release by one of his surrounding admirers.

C.T., Spectator, 16 January 1875

Medal Winner

A LADY FRIEND of mine had a very favourite cat, named 'Peter'. One night she left him in his usual sleeping-place, and went to her own room. Not long after she heard a noise at her door – scratching and other sounds, which she knew must come from the cat – and took no notice of it at first; but as it continued, she opened her door, upon which the cat immediately turned and walked down straight to the kitchen, followed by his mistress, who, to her dismay, saw that the legs of the table were on fire!

She started at once to the station of the fire brigade – not waiting for bonnet or shawl – (about five minutes' walk). The engine came and extinguished the fire, and the fire brigade presented the cat with a medal, which it wore always hung round its neck. This took place in Brighton.

The station of the fire brigade is in West Hill Road, where this story can be verified. The cause of the fire was traced to the fact of the fire in the grate having been raked out as usual, some of the hot cinders had reached the wood flooring, and the table was not far off.

Esther Wells, Spectator, 31 August 1899

Prisoner's Moggy

A FAVOURITE CAT of a young nobleman in the days of Queen Elizabeth was remarkable for its loyalty. For some political offence he had been shut up in prison, and had long pined in solitude, when he was startled by hearing a slight noise in the chimney.

On looking up, great was his surprise and delight to see his favourite cat bound over the hearth towards him, purring joyfully at the meeting. She had probably been shut up for some time before she had made her escape, and then she must have sought her master, traversing miles of steep and slippery roofs, along dangerous parapets, and through forests of chimney stacks, urged on by the strength of her attachment, and guided by a mysterious instinct, till she discovered the funnel which led into his prison chamber.

Certainly it was not by chance she made the discovery, nor was it exactly reason that conducted her to the spot. By whatever means she found it, we must regard the affectionate little creature as astonishingly clever.

Arthur Buckland, *Animals I Have Known*, 1858

Triple Catch

Fₗᵤff ᴡᴀs ᴀ ᴍɪɢʜᴛʏ huntress and on one occasion performed a feat which we think must be without parallel of its kind.

Her owners kept a large number of poultry, and the meal for them was kept in a long oak chest with a lid. One night the lid of the chest had been left open. Next morning, writes my informant, 'when I went for some meal, I heard a strange mingling of muffled growls and squeaks. I quickly looked inside the bin, and beheld old Fluff – with a mouse in her mouth and one under each front paw. She was determined not to lose one of her wonderful triple catch, and was quite miserable because she could not jump out of the bin with all three.'

What she would have done if left to herself it is impossible to say, for she was lifted out of the chest and two of the mice got away.

Finally, this champion fighter and record-breaking huntress distinguished herself in quite a different way. A sickly duckling having been given to her to mother, she lay down beside it in her basket, and 'purring with perfect content, allowed the little weakling to nestle up to her warm, soft body and contentedly go to sleep beside her own two kittens, who appeared quite pleased with their new yellow brother . . . In time it grew into quite a fine duck.'

Jennie Chappell, *Animals Worth Knowing*, S.W. Partridge, 1910

Clapham Beef

'PRIN' IS A magnificent animal, but withal a most dainty one, showing distinct disapproval of any meat not cooked in the especial way he likes – viz., roast. The cook, of whom he is very fond, determined to break this bad habit. Stewed or boiled meat was accordingly put ready for him, but, as he had often done before, he turned from it with disgust. However, this time no fish or roast was substituted.

For three days that saucer of meat was untouched, and no other food given. But on the fourth morning the cook was much rejoiced at finding the saucer empty. 'Prin' ran to meet her, and the good woman told her mistress how extra affectionate that repentant cat was that morning. He did enjoy his dinner of roast that day (no doubt served with a double amount of gravy). It was not till the pot

board under the dresser was cleaned on Saturday that r.
artfulness was brought to light.

There, in one of the stew pans, at the back behind the
others, was the contents of the saucer of stewed meat.
There was no other animal about the place, and the other
two servants were as much astonished as the cook at the
clever trick played on them by this terribly spoilt pet of
the house.

But cook was mortified at the thought of that saucer
of roast beef.

I know this story to be true, and I have known the cat
for the last nine or ten years. It lives at Clapham.

Faddist, *The Times*, 16 August 1895

A Sorrow Shared

THAT CATS expect those to whom they are attached to
sympathise with them in their sorrow, is shown by an
affecting story told by Dr Good, the author of the *Book
of Nature*.

He had a cat which used to sit at his elbow hour after
hour while he was writing, watching his hand moving over
the paper. At length Pussy had a kitten to take care of when
she became less constant in her attendance on her master.

One morning, however, she entered the room, and
leaping on the table, began to rub her furry side against

hand and pen, to attract his attention. He, supposing that she wished to be let out, opened the door; but instead of running forward, she turned round and looked earnestly at him, as though she had something to communicate. Being very busy, he shut the door upon her, and resumed his writing.

In less than an hour, the door having been opened again, he felt her rubbing against his feet; when, on looking down, he saw that she had placed close to them the dead body of her kitten, which had been accidentally killed, and which she had brought evidently that her kind master might mourn with her at her loss. She seemed satisfied when she saw him with the dead kitten in his hand, making inquiries as to how it had been killed; and when it was buried, believing that her master shared her sorrow, she gradually took comfort, and resumed her station at his side.

Observe how, in her sorrow, Pussy went to her best friend, for sympathy.

W.H.G. Kingston, *Stories of Animal Sagacity*, 1874

Riding High

MY BLACK LABRADOR, like most of its kind, will put up with almost any indignity – the molestations of children, relegation to the worst position by the fire.

An old cat had long taken the place closest to the fir
The Labrador did not mind. Then the cat died and a
kitten came.

Trying to assert himself, the dog lay in the warmest
place on the hearthrug; the kitten as she grew lay with
him. All seemed well; then the kitten as she grew yet further decided she needed more space. She lay half across
the Labrador's back and then fully across him.

One day fed up with this, the Labrador clambered up
and resigned himself to sleeping further away from the
heat he loved. But the fully grown kitten was not happy
with this arrangement. She followed him to the other side
of the room and then back to the fire. He lay down and
she lay down on him. He stood up and she clung to him,
climbing on to his back while he walked across the room.

He gave up the attempt to escape her and from then
on allowed her to lie as she pleased across his broad and
tolerant back.

Joe Fagin, *Scenes of my Youth*, 1900

Alarm Call

SOME PEOPLE we know have a cat of which they make
a great pet. He is not allowed upstairs at night, but one
night, after the family were all in bed, he went up, and
made such a noise outside the mother's bedroom door

t she got up, and tried to make him go away. But the cat would not go, and seemed so unhappy that at last his mistress went downstairs with him to see if she could find out what was the matter.

When she reached the hall, she found that somehow or other the front door had not been properly shut, and this is what he had come up to tell her.

Another friend remembers a cat her mother had who seemed to understand that illness meant inability to procure food. He had always been in the habit of proudly exhibiting to his mistress every rat he killed, and was never satisfied until she had seen his trophy and praised his cleverness. But during an illness she had, he more than once appeared with an offering of raw fish.

It was rather embarrassing to have puss jump on her bed and flop a cold wet sole or haddock on the counterpane, but it showed unmistakably that he understood that his mistress could no longer go out and hunt for her own meals; and the fact that he brought fish – the greatest delicacy he knew – instead of a common mouse or bird, seems to suggest that he considered that she ought to have the best obtainable.

The shop where his depredations were committed being some distance away, and across a broad road filled with traffic, made this feat the more remarkable, poor fellow!

His great love was accompanied by its too frequent shadow, jealousy. When the baby girl was born, he found

his place as chief pet filled by her, and when she grew
old enough to run about, his hatred of his rival was so
persistently shown by his spiteful scratching of her little
bare legs whenever he got the chance – a circumstance
painfully fresh in her recollection to the present day –
that his mistress was compelled, most regretfully, to have
him given away.

Jennie Chappell, *Animals Worth Knowing*, S.W. Partridge, 1910

Dog Imitator

THE MOST beautiful and best-trained cat I ever knew was
named Juno, and was brought up by a lady who was so
wise in all that related to the care and management of animals, that she might be quoted as authority on all points
of their nurture and breeding; and Juno, carefully trained
by such a mistress, was a standing example of the virtues
which may be formed in a cat by careful education.

Never was Juno known to be out of place, to take
her nap elsewhere than on her own appointed cushion,
to be absent at mealtimes, or, when the most tempting

dainties were in her power, to anticipate the proper time by jumping on the table to help herself.

In all her personal habits Juno was of a neatness unparalleled in cat history. The parlour of her mistress was always of a waxen and spotless cleanness, and Juno would have died sooner than violate its sanctity by any impropriety. She was a skilful mouser, and her sleek, glossy sides were a sufficient refutation of the absurd notion that a cat must be starved into a display of her accomplishments. Every rat, mouse, or ground mole that she caught was brought in and laid at the feet of her mistress for approbation.

But on one point her mind was dark. She could never be made to comprehend the great difference between fur and feathers, nor see why her mistress should gravely reprove her when she brought in a bird, and warmly commend when she captured a mouse.

After a while a little dog named Pero, with whom Juno had struck up a friendship, got into the habit of coming to her mistress's apartment at the hours when her modest meals were served, on which occasions Pero thought it would be a good idea to invite himself to make a third. He had a nice little trick of making himself amiable, by sitting up on his haunches, and making little begging gestures with his two forepaws, which so much pleased his hostess that sometimes he was fed before Juno.

Juno observed this in silence for some time; but at last a bright idea struck her, and, gravely rearing up on her haunches, she imitated Pero's gestures with her forepaws. Of course this carried the day, and secured her position.

Charles Dudley Warner, *Calvin*, 1870

Letting the Dog In

WE HAVE READ of a dog who, when he desired admittance to his home, would lie patiently waiting outside the door, till his housemate, the cat, came along, when she would lift the knocker and get them both let in. A friend of mine was passing along a street in the North of London, where bell-handles were fixed in the old-fashioned way to the area railings, and by pressure, pulled the bell-wire.

A cat came trotting along by the railings, and put her foot on the handle, which, of course, rang the bell. A woman came to the door almost immediately, and my friend remarked, 'I did not ring!'

'Oh, no!' replied the other, smiling. 'It was my cat, I know. She always rings the bell when she wants to come in.'

Jennie Chappell, *Animals Worth Knowing*, S.W. Partridge, 1910

Bun Counter

A FRIEND WAS one evening taking a cup of coffee at a small confectioner's, when a fine black cat came from behind the shop, ran along the counter, and with his paw dexterously knocked a bun off a stand on to the floor, when he seized and made off with it. My friend remarked to the mistress of the shop on what had happened.

'Yes,' replied the shopkeeper, 'he has a bun every evening for his supper, and if the proper time goes by, and I forget to give it to him, he comes and helps himself.'

Letter to the *Spectator*, June 1880

Knock Out

WHEN YOU SEE Pussy seated by the fireside, blinking her eyes, and looking very wise, you may often ask, 'I wonder what she can be thinking about.' Just then, probably, she is thinking about nothing at all; but if you were to turn her out of doors into the cold, and shut the door in her face, she would instantly begin to think, 'How can I best get in again?' And she would run round and round the house, trying to find a door or window open by which she might re-enter it.

I once heard of a cat which exerted a considerable amount of reason under these very circumstances. I am not quite certain of this Pussy's name, but it may possibly have been Deborah. The house where Deborah was born and bred is situated in the country, and there is a door with a small porch opening on a flower-garden. Very often when this door was shut, Deborah, or little Deb, as she may have been called, was left outside; and on such occasions she used to mew as loudly as she could to beg for admittance.

Occasionally she was not heard; but instead of running away, and trying to find some other home, she used – wise little creature that she was – patiently to ensconce herself in a corner of the windowsill, and wait till some person came to the house, who, on knocking at the door, found immediate attention. Many a day, no doubt, little Deb sat there on the windowsill and watched this proceeding, gazing at the knocker, and wondering what it had to do with getting the door open.

A month passed away, and little Deb grew from a kitten into a full-sized cat. Many a weary hour was passed in her corner. At length Deb arrived at the conclusion that if she could manage to make the knocker sound a rap-a-tap-tap on the door, the noise would summon the servant, and she would gain admittance as well as the guests who came to the house.

One day Deb had been shut out, when Mary, the maidservant, who was sitting industriously stitching away, heard a rap-a-tap at the front door, announcing the arrival, as she supposed, of a visitor. Putting down her work, she hurried to the door and lifted the latch; but no one was there except Deb, who at that moment leaped off the windowsill and entered the house. Mary looked along the road, up and down on either side, thinking that some person must have knocked and gone away; but no one was in sight. The following day the same thing happened, but it occurred several times before anyone suspected that Deb could possibly have lifted the knocker.

At length Mary told her mistress what she suspected, and one of the family hid in the shrubbery to watch Deb's proceedings. Deb was allowed to run out in the garden, and the door was closed. After a time, the little creature was seen to climb up on the windowsill, and then to rear herself on her hind feet, in an oblique position at the full stretch of her body, when, steadying herself with one front paw, with the other she raised the knocker; and Mary, who was on the Watch, instantly ran to the door and let her in.

Miss Deb's knock now became as well known to the servant as that of any other member of the family, and, no doubt to her great satisfaction, it usually met with prompt attention.

Not only must Deb have exercised reason and reflection, as well as imitation, but a considerable amount of perseverance; for probably she made many vain attempts before she was rewarded with success.

Some Scotch ladies told me of a cat they had when young, brought by their grandfather from Archangel, Russia, which, under the same circumstances, used to reach up to the latch of the front door of a house in the country, and to rattle away on it till admitted. I have seen a cat which the same ladies now possess make a similar attempt.

Does it not occur to you that you may take a useful lesson from little Pussy, and when you have an object to gain, a task to perform, think over the matter, and exert yourself to the utmost till you have accomplished it!

W.H.G. Kingston, *Stories of Animal Sagacity*, 1874

Rancher

WHILE STAYING in the Rocky Mountains in Northern Colorado, I witnessed an example of fatherly affection in a tomcat, which I feel sure you will be interested to hear of. This cat had adopted two motherless kittens; he slept with them at night, guarded them in the daytime, and always superintended their meals, in which latter he showed great unselfishness.

For the hostess of the ranch was in the habit of feeding the kittens out of a small bowl of milk laid on the floor, into which they at once would plunge their heads; meanwhile 'Kitty Grey', the old tomcat – quite aware that there was not room for his own great head in it, too – would sit by, complacently watching them, nor move till they had finished, except when his hunger was very keen, and then he would dip his paw in now and again and lick it.

This was the case when I saw him; and I shall not readily forget the sight of that large grey-and-white cat walking demurely round the bowl to see where he could best insert his paw without disturbing the kittens, and then, with his head much on one side, dipping it delicately in and out, until they had quite finished, when he at once fell to and drank up the remainder.

L.C.P., *San Jose News*, February 1885

Latch Claw

THE DOMESTIC cat is a wonderful animal; but I fancy your readers are not aware that they can open doors.

I have one that always opens the back door himself. His method is simple: he springs up to a ledge close to the latch and puts one paw on the latch, the weight causing it to rise, when 'Topsy' jumps down and walks in.

We made it harder for him to do it by removing the ledge, but he sprang from the ground, dug the claws of one paw into the wood by the latch long enough to get the other paw onto the latch itself and push down. He then retracted the claws stuck in the wood, fell gently to earth and pushed the now unlatched door open.

I would not believe it for a long time, but now I can account for many missing articles of food.

The Times, 30 May 1885

Cat Burglar

No STRONGER evidence of the intelligence of the cat is to be found than an instance narrated to me by my friend, Mrs F, and for which I can vouch.

A lady, Miss P, who was a governess in her family, had previously held the same position in that of Lord Tottenham in Ireland. While there a cat became very strongly attached to her. Though allowed to enter the schoolroom and dining-room, where she was fed and petted, the animal never came into the lady's bedroom; nor was she, indeed, accustomed to go into that part of the house at any time.

One night, however, after retiring to rest, Miss P was disturbed by the gentle but incessant mewing of the cat at her bedroom door. At first she was not inclined to pay attention to the cat's behaviour, but the perseverance of the animal, and a peculiarity in the tones of her voice, at length induced her to open the door.

The cat, on this, bounded forward, and circled round her rapidly, looking up in her face, mewing expressively. Miss P, thinking that the cat had only taken a fancy to pay her a visit, refastened the door, intending to let her remain in the room; but this did not appear to please Pussy at all.

She sprang back to the door, mewing more loudly than before; then she came again to the lady, and then went to the door, as if asking her to follow.

'What is it you want?' exclaimed Miss P. 'Well, go away, if you do not wish to stay!' and she opened the door; but the cat, instead of going, recommenced running to and fro between the door and her friend, continuing to mew as she looked up into her face.

Miss P's attention was now attracted by a peculiar noise, as if proceeding from the outside of one of the windows on the ground floor. A few moments more convinced her that some persons were attempting to force an entrance.

Instantly throwing a shawl around her, she hurried along the passage, the cat gliding by her side, purring now in evident contentment, to Lord T's bedroom door, where her knock was quickly answered, and an explanation given.

The household was soon aroused; bells were rung, lights fitted about, servants hurried here and there; and persons watching from the windows distinctly saw several men making off with all speed, and scrambling over an adjacent wall.

It was undoubtedly owing to the sagacity of the cat that the house was preserved from midnight robbery, and the inmates probably from some fearful outrage.

She must have reasoned that the intruders had no business there; while her reason and affection combined induced her to warn her best friend of the threatened danger. She may have feared, also, that anyone else in the house would have driven her heedlessly away.

May we not believe that this reasoning power was given to the dumb animal for the protection of the family against evil-doers? I might give you many instances of beneficent purposes being carried out by equally simple and apparently humble agencies.

W.H.G. Kingston, *Stories of Animal Sagacity*, 1874

Bell Ringer

I KNEW A CAT that lived in a nunnery in France. She had observed that when a certain bell was rung, all the inmates assembled for their meals, when she also received her food. One day she was shut up in a room by herself when she heard the bell ring. In vain she attempted to get out; she could not open the door, the window was too high to reach.

At length, after some hours' imprisonment, the door was opened. Off she hurried to the place where she expected to find her dinner, but none was there. She was very hungry, and hunger is said to sharpen the wits. She knew where the rope hung which pulled the bell in the belfry.

'Now, when that bell rings I generally get my supper,' she thought, as she ran towards the rope. It hung down temptingly within her reach – a good thick rope. She sprang upon it. It gave a pleasant tinkle. She jerked harder and harder, and the bell rang louder and louder. 'Now I shall get my supper, though I have lost my dinner,' she thought as she pulled away.

The nuns hearing the bell ring at so unusual an hour, came hurrying into the belfry, wondering what was the matter, when what was their surprise to see the cat turned bell-ringer.

They puzzled their heads for some time, till the lay sister who generally gave the cat her meals recollected that she had not been present at dinner-time; and thus the mystery was solved, and Pussy rewarded for her exertions by having her supper brought to her without delay.

Manchester Guardian, January 1870

Remorseful

HERE IS THE story of a cat and a bird. Two young ladies dwelt together, one the owner of a canary, which she petted and played with; the other was the mistress of a beautiful cat, which was nursed and patted and petted also. They were a happy and united family.

The owner of the cat went abroad for a time, and pussy grew sad and melancholy, and at last became jealous of the bird, which was daily petted as usual, while she was sadly neglected.

Pussy could not, and would not, stand this treatment; her jealousy grew day by day till at last, in a fit of rage, she made a dash at the little bird and tore him limb from limb. Then seized by remorse she fled, but the owner of the bird was frantic, and she beat the cat and mourned for her bird; and the owner of the cat when she heard of the catastrophe shed sad tears, not, indeed, because the bird was dead, but because her pussy had been beaten; and so the peace of that happy family was destroyed for a time.

Pussy, overwhelmed with remorse at the crime she had committed, was found the next day curled up and asleep in the little bird's cage. Now, the problem for psychologists required to be solved is, why did that cat go into to the cage?

The only solution that suggests itself to those persons concerned is, that by going there she thought she might regain the favour of the mistress whose happiness she had so ruthlessly destroyed, by taking the place of the bird, and so, perhaps, in due course be changed into a little petted bird herself.

Catalonia, *Newcastle Journal*, 19 October 1895

Lights Out

A LARGE AND very handsome Persian cat came to my knowledge recently while staying at Bar Harbour, Maine. The maid who fed Buff and for whom he seemed to have most affection, was in the habit of putting out the lamps in the parlour, where Buff slept on a rug in the corner, after we retired.

He is tall enough, when standing on his hind feet, to rattle the knob of the door with his paw, and this is his usual way of asking to be let in.

Just as Jennie was going to bed, she heard this sound, and when she opened the door, he mewed and ran toward the stairs; she followed him to the parlour, and perceived at once it was to put out the lamps she was called. As soon as she had done this, he laid down content. How much reasoning did this action on the cat's part imply?

M.S.T., *The Times*, 26 September 1895

Chapter Three

CRAZY CATS

Two-legged Race

A CAT POSSESSED by the writer in earliest childhood was accustomed to follow her short-socked legs with very strange intent. He acquired the queer habit, whenever she ran down the long garden path, of following close behind to pat first one leg and then the other, with velvet paws.

How he contrived to do this, no one could ever quite see, but it seemed as though he ran upon his hind feet only, for the front ones seemed continually occupied, the right one in patting the right leg of the child and the left one the left leg, all the time she ran.

She was but four or five years old when this took place, but perfectly remembers being called and told to run down the garden, that visitors might be amused by

67

Tiny's performance, and also recollects the unfailingly gentle touch of the playful little paws.

Jennie Chappell, *Animals Worth Knowing*, S.W. Partridge, 1910

Worm Hunter

A CAT OF MY acquaintance takes a delight in sitting sometimes for over an hour upon the flower-bed, watching for worms to come out. It 'often scratches the earth with its forepaws, which causes the worms to come to the surface . . . As soon as the worms rise, she simply pats them and they quickly sink down again. Sometimes even in a heavy shower of rain the cat will sit out on the flower-bed and carry on this diversion.

Countryside, March 1886

Slightly Foxed

YOUR INTERESTING article on cats prompts me to send you the following entertaining instance of affection between a 'domestic sphinx' and its natural enemy, the fox.

The cat in question, which hails from the Isle of Man, is apparently to all intents and purposes in love with a young fox inhabiting the same house, and the 'spooning' that goes on between them is comic in the extreme. On one occasion, in my presence, the fox feeling dissatisfied or aggrieved at something or other that was taking place, vented his feelings in a long, strange howl.

The cat, who was on the hearthrug, turned her head, and gazed with a wistful, sympathetic expression at her suffering friend for some seconds; at last, unable to listen to his weeping any longer, she sprang upon him, put her paws round his neck, and kissed his cheek with her lips.

This occurred twice, the second time the fox responding to her caresses by tickling her back, in the tenderest manner conceivable. I am not aware whether the exhibition of emotion or of reason is the less compatible with the theory of animals as automatons; in either case, however, I think the fact I have described is not wholly unworthy the attention of those who have, before now, defended that doctrine in your correspondence columns.

Frederick H. Balfour, *Spectator*, 6 April 1878

Crazy

LIVING IN the suburbs, we are infested by cats of all kinds, and are perpetually driving them away, aided by our own long-haired black Persian, who pursues them off the premises with hair and tail standing wildly erect, and presenting a most alarming appearance.

We feel that this violent demonstration must be a joke, as the same cat constantly carries the remains of her own dinner about twenty-five yards, across an open space and up some steps, to feed the identical animals she has driven off an hour or two previously.

A.E.L., *Spectator*, 16 August 1890

Spiky

Many years ago I was living in a house where a hedgehog was kept for the destruction of black beetles.

I had heard that hedgehogs would eat mice; and one day finding the cat playing with a mouse she had caught, I took it from her and gave it to the hedgehog, who immediately proceeded to devour it.

The cat was at first furious, and began to claw at the hedgehog, who, however, only elevated its spines, and quietly went on with its meal, and the cat soon desisted from the attempt to recover her lost prey.

The curious part of the story is what followed. For weeks afterwards, whenever the cat caught a mouse, she went in search of the hedgehog, and did not rest until she found it, and had placed the mouse where the hedgehog could secure it.

I cannot say how often this was done, but am sure it was not fewer than half-a-dozen times. Perhaps some of your readers may be able to define the motive which induced these repeated acts of self-denial.

J.S., *Spectator*, 30 August 1890

Ganging Up

A FRIEND LATELY told me of a ferocious cat. This cat lived in the same house with a dog, with which she was on the friendliest terms. But there was also a little kitten, of which she was not the mother, and towards which she was anything but gentle.

The dog, too, was a hater of all cats except his friend, and very fond of driving them. Well, one day the dog attacked this poor little kitten, and was on the point of seizing it by the throat and putting an end to it, when the small creature jumped upon the table, and as he was unable to follow he did not know what to do, until he bethought him of fetching his friend, the grown-up cat.

Accordingly, he went in search, and soon returned with her, when she very quickly jumped on to the table too, and actually had the wickedness to push the poor little thing down to the dog, which would then very speedily have made an end of it, had not the children of the family come in and rescued their pet.

The Clan of the Cats, Seeley, Jackson & Halliday, 1877

Cat's Title

THE POET Robert Southey was an ardent lover of cats. He wrote to a friend, announcing the death of one: 'Alas, Grosvenor, this day poor Rumpel was found dead, after as long and happy a life as cat could wish for, if cats form wishes on that subject.

'His full titles were: The Most Noble, the Archduke Rumpelstiltzchen, Marcus Macbum, Earl Tomlefnagne, Baron Raticide, Waowhler and Scratch.

'There should be a court-mourning in Catland, and if the Dragon (your pet cat) wear a black ribbon round his neck, or a band of crape *à la militaire* round one of his forepaws it will be but a becoming mark of respect.'

Then the poet adds, 'I believe we are each and all, servants included, more sorry for his loss, or, rather, more affected by it, than any of us would like to confess.'

Helen Winslow, *Concerning Cats*, 1900

Animal Magic

Frank Buckland, the Victorian naturalist, inventor and for many years chief inspector of her majesty's fisheries, had a house full of animals. As a boy at Winchester school he kept hares and frogs and tortoises, mice, rats, cats, and even eels in a bath.

By the time he'd reached middle age he had a house in London filled to bursting with live, dead, caged, uncaged, dying, stuffed and pickled animals from all over the world. He presided over this menagerie with the help of a large ginger cat to which he was devoted. The cat helped him concentrate when he was dissecting, he claimed, and it calmed him when he became agitated if an experiment failed, or the promised delivery of a new specimen proved false.

A visitor was as likely to meet a monkey on the stairs, or an armadillo, as a cat or dog. For years a dead gorilla languished in a large barrel filled with rum while a giant sunfish sprawled in a vast saucer of formaldehyde. In the basement of the house, Buckland dissected any animal that had died and, generally speaking, he then cooked it and shared the dish with his cat.

One of his chief claims to fame and legacies to the modern world was the Buckland Dining Club which still meets today – a typical menu will consist of sea slug followed by dormouse on toast.

But in addition to his passion for animals of all sorts, Buckland had a passion for new inventions and chief among these was the railway – as often as he was able, Buckland would take the train and, of course, his favourite pets, but especially his cat, always accompanied him.

Buckland's most famous journey began, as he later recalled, on a foggy autumn morning when he presented himself at St Pancras Station ticket office.

He was taking with him on the journey a monkey, which proved a bit of a stumbling block to the booking office clerk, who carefully went through the schedule of charges for the carriage of animals.

'Cows is horses,' at length he said, 'and so is donkeys. Cats is dogs and fowls is likewise and so is monkeys. That 'ere animal will have to go as a dawg.'

'And what about this?' said an indignant Buckland, pulling a tortoise out of his pocket.

Once more the schedule was perused.

'They are nothing,' said the clerk with some scorn after a few moments. 'We don't charge nothing for them. They're an insek.'

While all this was going on the cat, its head peeping out of a large Gladstone bag, maintained an air not unlike that of an unusually patient vicar.

George Bompas, *Life of Frank Buckland*, 1885

Snow Play

I RECENTLY SAW a domestic cat deliberately kicking snow off a window ledge on to dog's head. The dog and the cat were old enemies and the dog was clearly waiting below the window in the hope that the cat would be foolish enough to come down. Instead, every now and then she executed a rapid scuffling with her paws and a shower of powdery snow hit the upturned face of the dog. She then gazed down in satisfaction as the dog shook its head and became increasingly and impotently enraged.

E.F. Williamson, *The Times*, 1888

Drumming Hare

MR COWPER the poet had beside two dogs, two gold-finches and two canaries, five rabbits, three hares, two guinea pigs, a squirrel a magpie a jay, a starling and a cat.

One evening the cat giving one of the hares a sound box on the ear, the hare ran after her and having caught her punished her by drumming on her back with her two feet as hard as drumsticks till the creature would actually have been killed had not Mrs Unwin rescued her.

Lady Hesketh, *Cowper's Cat*, 1812

Dynasties

DYNASTIES OF cats, as numerous as those of the Egyptian kings, succeeded each other in my dwelling.

One after another they were swept away by accident, by flight, by death. All were loved and regretted: but life is made up of oblivion, and the memory of cats dies out like the memory of men. My old grey cat always took my part against my parents, and used to bite my mother's legs when she presumed to reprove me.

Childebrand. Now I considered Childebrand a very fine name indeed, Merovingian, mediaeval, and Gothic, and vastly preferable to Agamemnon, Achilles, Ulysses, or any Greek name whatsoever. Romanticism was the fashion of my early days: I have no doubt the people of classical times called their cats Hector, Ajax, or Patroclus. Childebrand was a splendid cat of common kind, tawny and striped with black, like the hose of Saltabadil in *Le roi s'amuse*. With his large, green, almond-shaped eyes, and his symmetrical stripes, there was something tiger-like about him that pleased me.

Childebrand had the honour of figuring in some verses I wrote. Childebrand was brought in to make a good rhyme for Rembrandt.

I come next to Madame Théophile, a red cat, with a white breast, a pink nose, and blue eyes, whom I called by that name because we were on terms of the closest intimacy. She slept at the foot of my bed: she sat on the arm of my chair while I wrote: she came down into the garden and gravely walked about with me: she was present at all my meals, and frequently intercepted a choice morsel on its way from my plate to my mouth.

One day a friend, who was going away for a short time, brought me his parrot to be taken care of during his absence. The bird, finding itself in a strange place, climbed up to the top of its perch by the aid of its beak, and rolled its eyes (as yellow as the nails in my armchair) in a rather frightened manner, also moving the white membranes that formed its eyelids.

Madame Théophile had never seen a parrot, and she regarded the creature with manifest surprise. While remaining as motionless as a cat mummy from Egypt in its swathing bands, she fixed her eyes upon the bird with a look of profound meditation, summoning up all the notions of natural history that she had picked up in the yard, in the garden, and on the roof.

The shadow of her thoughts passed over her changing eyes, and we could plainly read in them the conclusion to which her scrutiny led, 'Decidedly this is a green chicken.'

This result attained, the next proceeding of Madame Théophile was to jump off the table from which she had made her observations, and lay herself flat on the ground in a corner of the room, exactly in the attitude of a panther watching the gazelles as they come down to drink at a lake. The parrot followed the movements of the cat with feverish anxiety: it ruffled its feathers, rattled its chain, lifted one of its feet and shook the claws, and rubbed its beak against the edge of its trough. Instinct told it that the cat was an enemy and meant mischief.

The cat's eyes were now fixed upon the bird with fascinating intensity, and they said in perfectly intelligible language, which the poor parrot distinctly understood, 'This chicken ought to be good to eat, although it is green.' We watched the scene with great interest, ready to interfere at need.

Madame Théophile was creeping nearer and nearer almost imperceptibly; her pink nose quivered, her eyes were half-closed, her contractile claws moved in and out of their velvet sheaths, slight thrills of pleasure ran along her backbone at the idea of the meal she was about to make. Such novel and exotic food excited her appetite.

All in an instant her back took the shape of a bent bow, and with a vigorous and elastic bound she sprang upon the perch. The parrot, seeing its danger, squawked in a deep voice.

This utterance so terrified the cat that she sprang backwards. The blare of a trumpet, the crash and smash of a pile of plates flung to the ground, a pistol shot fired off by her ear, could not have frightened her more thoroughly. All her ornithological ideas were overthrown.

Then might we, the observers, read in the physiognomy of Madame Théophile, 'This is not a bird, it is a gentleman; it talks.' The parrot shrieked again in a deafening voice, for it had perceived that its best means of defence was the terror aroused by its speech. The cat cast a glance at me which was full of questioning, but as my response was not satisfactory, she promptly hid herself under the bed, and from that refuge she could not be induced to stir during the whole of the day.

People who are not accustomed to live with animals, and who, like Descartes, regard them as mere machines, will think that I lend unauthorized meanings to the acts of the quadruped, but I have only faithfully translated their ideas into human language.

The next day Madame Théophile plucked up courage and made another attempt, which was similarly repulsed. From that moment she gave it up, accepting the bird as a variety of man.

This dainty and charming animal was extremely fond of perfumes, especially of patchouli and the scent exhaled by India shawls. She was also very fond of music, and would listen, sitting on a pile of music books, while the fair singers who came to try my piano filled his room with melody. All the time Madame Théophile would evince great pleasure. She was, however, made nervous by certain notes, and at the high la she would tap the singer's mouth with her paw. This was very amusing, and my visitors delighted in making the experiment. It never failed; the dilettante in fun was not to be deceived.

The rule of the White Dynasty belonged to a later epoch, and was inaugurated in the person of a pretty little kitten as white as a powder puff, who came from Havana. On account of his spotless whiteness he was called Pierrot; but when he grew up this name was very properly magnified into Don-Pierrot-de-Navarre, which was far more majestic, and suggested grandee-ism.

Don-Pierrot-de-Navarre shared in the life of the household with the enjoyment of quiet fireside friendship that is characteristic of cats. He had his own place near the fire, and there he would sit with a convincing air of comprehension of all that was talked of and of interest in it; he followed the looks of the speakers, and uttered little sounds toward them as though he, too, had objections to make and opinions to give upon the literary subjects which were most frequently discussed.

He was very fond of books, and when he found one open on a table he would lie down on it, turn over the edges of the leaves with his paws, and after a while fall asleep, for all the world as if he had been reading a fashionable novel.

He was deeply interested in my writing, too; the moment I took up my pen he would jump upon the desk, and follow the movement of the penholder with the gravest attention, making a little movement with his head at the beginning of each line. Sometimes he would try to take the pen out of my hand.

Don-Pierrot-de-Navarre never went to bed until I had come in. He would wait for me just inside the outer door and rub himself to my legs, his back in an arch, with a glad and friendly purring. Then he would go on before me, preceding me with a page-like air, and I have no doubt, if I had asked him, he would have carried the candlestick. Having thus conducted me to my bedroom, he would wait quietly while I undressed, and then jump on my bed, take my neck between his paws, gently rub my nose with his own, and lick me with his small, pink tongue, as rough as a file, uttering all the time little inarticulate cries, which expressed as clearly as any words could do his perfect satisfaction at having me with him again.

After these caresses he would perch himself on the back of the bedstead and sleep there, carefully balanced, like a bird on a branch. When I awoke, he would come down and lie beside me until I got up.

Pierrot was as strict as a concierge in his notions of the proper hour for all good people to return to their homes. He did not approve of anything later than midnight. In those days we had a little society among friends, which we called The Four Candles, the light in our place of meeting being restricted to four candles in silver candlesticks, placed at the four corners of the tables. Sometimes the talk became so animated that I forgot all about time, and twice or three times Pierrot sat up for me until two o'clock in the morning. After a while, however, my conduct in this respect displeased him, and he retired to rest without me. I was touched by this mute protest against my innocent dissipation, and thenceforth came home regularly at twelve o'clock.

Nevertheless, Pierrot cherished the memory of my offence for some time; he waited to test the reality of my repentance, but when he was convinced that my conversion was sincere, he deigned to restore me to his good graces, and resumed his nocturnal post in the anteroom.

To gain the friendship of a cat is a difficult thing. The cat is a philosophical, methodical, quiet animal, tenacious of its own habits, fond of order and cleanliness, and it does not lightly confer its friendship. If you are worthy of its affection, a cat will be your friend, but never your slave. He keeps his free will, though he loves, and he will not do for you what he thinks unreasonable; but if he once gives himself to you, it is with such absolute confidence, such fidelity of affection. He makes himself the companion of your hours of solitude, melancholy, and toil. He remains for whole evenings on your knee, uttering his contented purr, happy to be with you, and forsaking the company of animals of his own species.

In vain do melodious mewings on the roof invite him to one of those cat parties in which fish bones play the part of tea and cakes; he is not to be tempted away from you. Put him down and he will jump up again, with a sort of cooing sound that is like a gentle reproach; and sometimes he will sit upon the carpet in front of you, looking at you with eyes so melting, so caressing, and so human, that they almost frighten you, for it is impossible to believe that a soul is not there.

Don-Pierrot-de-Navarre had a sweetheart of the same race and of as snowy a whiteness as himself. The ermine would have looked yellow by the side of Seraphita, for so this lovely creature was named, in honour of Balzac's Swedenborgian romance.

Seraphita was of a dreamy and contemplative disposition. She would sit on a cushion for hours together, quite motionless, not asleep, and following with her eyes, in a rapture of attention, sights invisible to mere mortals. Caresses were agreeable to her, but she returned them in a very reserved manner, and only in the case of persons whom she favoured with her rarely accorded esteem.

She was fond of luxury, and it was always upon the handsomest easy-chair, or the rug that would best show off her snowy fur, that she would surely be found. She devoted a great deal of time to her toilet, her glossy coat was carefully smoothed every morning. She washed herself with her paw, and licked every atom of her fur with her pink tongue until it shone like new silver. When any one touched her, she instantly effaced all trace of the contact; she could not endure to be tumbled. An idea of aristocracy was suggested by her elegance and distinction, and among her own people she was a duchess at least. She delighted in perfumes, would stick her nose into bouquets, bite scented handkerchiefs with little spasms of pleasure, and walk about among the scent bottles on the toilet table, smelling at their stoppers; no doubt, she would have used the powder puff if she had been permitted.

Such was Seraphita, and never did cat more amply justify a poetic name. I must mention here that, in the days of the White Dynasty, I was also the happy possessor of a family of white rats, and that the cats, always supposed to be their natural, invariable, and irreconcilable enemies, lived in perfect harmony with my pet rodents. The rats never showed the slightest distrust of the cats, nor did the cats ever betray their confidence.

Don-Pierrot de-Navarre was very much attached to them. He would sit close to their cage and observe their gambols for hours together, and if by any chance the door of the room in which they were left was shut, he would scratch and mew gently until someone came to open it and allow him to rejoin his little white friends, who would often come out of the cage and sleep close to him. Seraphita, who was of a more reserved and disdainful temper, and who disliked the musky odour of the white rats, took no part in their games; but she never did them any harm, and would let them pass before her without putting out a claw.

Don-Pierrot-de-Navarre, who came from Havana, required a hothouse temperature: and this he always had in his own apartments. The house was, however, surrounded by extensive gardens, divided by railings, through and over which cats could easily climb, and in those gardens were trees inhabited by a great number of birds.

Pierrot would frequently take advantage of an open door to get out of an evening and go a-hunting through the wet grass and flower-beds; and, as his mewing under the windows when he wanted to get in again did not always awaken the sleepers in the house, he frequently had to stay out until morning. His chest was delicate, and one very chilly night he caught a cold which rapidly developed into phthisis.

At the end of a year of coughing, poor Don Pierrot had wasted to a skeleton, and his coat, once so silky, was a dull, harsh white. His big, transparent eyes looked unnaturally large in his shrunken face: the pink of his little nose had faded, and he dragged himself slowly along the sunny side of the wall with a melancholy air, looking at the yellow autumnal leaves as they danced and whirled in the wind.

Nothing is so touching as a sick animal: it submits to suffering with such gentle and sad resignation. We did all in our power to save Pierrot: a skilful doctor came to see him, felt his pulse, sounded his lungs, and ordered him ass's milk. He drank the prescribed beverage very readily out of his own especial china saucer. For hours together he lay stretched upon my knee, like the shadow of a sphinx. I felt his spine under my fingertips like the beads of a rosary, and he tried to respond to my caresses by a feeble purr that resembled a death-rattle.

On the day of his death he was lying on his side panting, and suddenly, with a supreme effort, he rose and came to me. His large eyes were opened wide, and he gazed at me with a look of intense supplication, a look that seemed to say, 'Save me, save me, you, who are a man.' Then he made a few faltering steps, his eyes became glassy, and he fell down, uttering so lamentable a cry, so dreadful and full of anguish, that I was struck dumb and motionless with horror. He was buried at the bottom of the garden under a white rose tree, which still marks the place of his sepulchre.

Three years later Seraphita died, and was buried by the side of Don Pierrot. With her the White Dynasty became extinct, but not the family. This snow-white couple had three children, who were as black as ink. Let anyone explain that mystery who can. The kittens were born in the early days of the great renown of Victor Hugo's *Les Misérables*, when everybody was talking of the new masterpiece, and the names of the personages in it were in every mouth.

The two little male creatures were called Enjolras and Gavroche, and their sister received the name of Éponine.

They were very pretty and I trained them to run after a little ball of paper and bring it back to me when I threw it into the corner of the room. In time they would follow the ball up to the top of the bookcase, or fish for it behind boxes or in the bottom of china vases with their dainty little paws.

As they grew up they came to disdain those frivolous amusements, and assumed the philosophical and meditative quiet which is the true temperament of the cat. To the eyes of the careless and indifferent observer, three black cats are just three black cats, but those who are really acquainted with animals know that their physiognomy is as various as that of the human race.

I was perfectly well able to distinguish between these little faces, as black as Harlequin's mask, and lighted up by disks of emerald with golden gleams. Enjolras, who was much the handsomest of the three, was remarkable for his broad, leonine head and full whiskers, strong shoulders, and a superb feathery tail. There was something theatrical and pretentious in his air, like the posing of a popular actor. His movements were slow, undulatory, and majestic: so circumspect was he about where he set his feet down that he always seemed to be walking among glass and china. His disposition was by no means stoical, and he was much too fond of food to have been approved of by his namesake.

The temperate and austere Enjolras would certainly have said to him, as the angel said to Swedenborg, 'You eat too much.' I encouraged his gastronomical tastes, and Enjolras attained a very unusual size and weight.

Gavroche was a remarkably knowing cat, and looked it. He was wonderfully active, and his twists, twirls, and tumbles were very comic. He was of a Bohemia temperament, and fond of low company. Thus he would occasionally compromise the dignity of his descent from the illustrious Don-Pierrot-de-Navarre, grandee Spain of the first class, and the Marquesa Dona Seraphita, of aristocratic and disdainful bearing. He would sometimes return from his expeditions to the street, accompanied by gaunt, starved companions, whom he had picked up in his wandering and he would stand complacently by while they bolted the contents of his plate food in a violent hurry and in dread of dispersion by a broomstick or a shower of water. I was sometimes tempted to say to Gavroche, 'A nice lot of friends you pick up,' but I refrained, for, after all, it was an amiable weakness: he might have eaten his dinner all by himself.

The interesting Éponine was more slender and graceful than her brothers, and she was an extraordinarily sensitive, nervous, and electric animal. She was passionately attached to me, and she would do the honours of my hermitage with perfect grace and propriety. When the bell rang, she hastened to the door, received the visitors, conducted them to the salon, made them take seats, talked to them – yes, talked, with little coos, murmurs, and cries quite unlike the language which cats use among themselves, and which bordered on the articulate speech of man.

What did she say? She said quite plainly: 'Don't be impatient: look at the pictures, or talk with me, if I amuse you. My master is coming down.'

On my appearing she would retire discreetly to an armchair or the corner of the piano, and listen to the conversation without interrupting it, like a well-bred animal accustomed to good society.

Éponine's intelligence, fine disposition, and sociability led to her being elevated by common consent to the dignity of a person, for reason, superior instinct, plainly governed her conduct. That dignity conferred on her the right to eat at table like a person, and not in a corner on the floor, from a saucer, like an animal.

Éponine had a chair by my side at breakfast and dinner, but in consideration of her size she was privileged to place her forepaws on the table. Her place was laid, without a knife and fork, indeed, but with a glass, and she went regularly through dinner, from soup to dessert, awaiting her turn to be helped, and behaving with a quiet propriety which most children might imitate with advantage.

At the first stroke of the bell she would appear, and when I came into the dining-room she would be at her post, upright in her chair, her forepaws on the edge of the tablecloth, and she would present her smooth forehead to be kissed, like a well-bred little girl who was affectionately polite to relatives and old people. When we had friends to dine with us, Éponine always knew that company was expected. She would look at her place, and if a knife, fork, and spoon lay near her plate she would immediately turn away and seat herself on the piano-stool, her invariable refuge.

Let those who deny the possession of reason to animals explain, if they can, this little fact, apparently so simple, but which contains a world of induction. From the presence near her plate of those implements which only man can use, the observant and judicious cat concluded that she ought on this occasion to give way to a guest, and she hastened to do so. She was never mistaken: only, when the visitor was a person whom she knew and liked, she would jump on his knee and coax him for a bit off his plate with her graceful caresses. She survived her brothers, and was my dear companion for several years . . . Such is the chronicle of the Black Dynasty.

Théophile Gautier, *My Private Menagerie*, 1845

Duck Surprise

CATS WILL OFTEN look after orphaned pups, leverets and even the young of birds, so strong is their maternal instinct. But it is rare for a cat to push out the real mother so that she can take over.

In a certain kitchen a duck and her ducklings were placed in a basket, lined with flannel, by the kitchen fire. A cat lay there, and used, as cats often do, to sleep away most of her days enjoying the warmth.

But when this basket was introduced the cat roused up, and began watching its little inmates with great interest. Nor was it long before she took a resolution. She would have those ducklings — they were pretty downy little things; she would be their mother, and the old duck should be spared the trouble. So, going up to the basket, she pushed the old mother out – not roughly, but gently — and having got rid of her she got in herself, and spread her body over the little things, keeping them warm, as she had noticed the mother do, and always drawing them back when they tried to get away.

Countryman, Spring 1935

Frog Friend

AN EXTRAORDINARY friendship was once formed between a cat and a frog.

The frog had made his way into a house through a hole in the kitchen wall, and was fond of sitting before the fire.

He became a great friend of the old cat, and would often nestle himself under her fur, she all the while making no objection, but seeming quite fond of her strange companion.

When the frog hopped across the lawn the cat guarded him. When he hopped back into the house she accompanied him. When he hopped into the garden pond she became agitated and ran round the edge peering into the water until he hopped out again and returned to the house.

A frog and a cat becoming friends is indeed strange, but I have also heard of cats befriending rats, squirrels, pheasant poults and even mice!

J.H., *Spectator*, April 1877

Parrot Fashion

At Northrepps Hall, near Cromer, the seat of the late Sir Fowell Buxton, a large colony of parrots and macaws had been established and for whom a home had been provided near the house in a large open aviary, with hutches for them to lay in.

But the birds as a rule preferred the woods, at any rate during the summer, only coming home at feeding time, when, on the well-known tinkling of the spoon on the tin containing their food, a large covey of gaily plumaged birds came fluttering down to the feeding place, presenting a sight not often to be seen in England.

The hutches being then practically deserted, a cat found one of them a convenient place to kitten in. While the mother cat was away foraging, one of the female parrots paid a chance visit to the place, and finding the young kittens in her nest, at once adopted them as her own, and was found by Lady Buxton's man covering her strange adopted children with her wings.

Whether this practice was continued, as in Mr. Egerton's case, or only adopted on this one occasion, I cannot say. May I be permitted to add another count to the indictment against the 'odious' and 'odorous' black beetle, or 'cockroach', formulated in your amusing article on 'Household Pests'? The wretched creature is very fond of the paste with which in former days (one seldom sees them now) the paper titles of books were affixed to their backs. When living on the Undercliff of the Isle of Wight, my house swarmed with these foul insects. They drowned themselves in one's milk, swam in one's soup, and nibbled one's pastry. They even invaded our beds; nor was it conducive to a night's calm repose, on turning down the bedclothes, to see one or more of these wretches scurrying away over the sheets.

We laid traps for them – a very clever dodge – by filling soup plates with beer, with a fringe of split sticks resting on the ground, by which they might climb, and after having drunk their fill, lose their heads, tumble in and be drowned. The abundance of these pests may be gathered when I say that one morning we found between twenty and thirty of various ages, sizes, and colours drowned in the beer in our own bedroom. My study having the kitchen fireplace behind it, was a favourite resort for these horrible insects. On the shelves by the fireplace there were a number of volumes with the white paper labels I have spoken of. These labels, to my annoyance, I found gradually disappearing; not peeling off, but wasting away in comminuted fragments.

For some time, this was a mystery to me; at last, while I sat writing late at the other side of the room, I was conscious of slight rustlings and scrapings by the fireplace, and on examining my bookshelves I found the cockroaches making their supper on the backs of my books.

Subsequent alterations in the house removed the kitchen, and the loss of the warmth which cockroaches so much delight in made them shift their quarters, and the injury to my library ceased; and the kitchen being in a remote part of the house, their visits to the bedrooms became less frequent. Like the writer of the article, I tried a hedgehog. The worthy animal did his best. He devoured cockroaches to repletion, an over-full meal sometimes making him almost a greater nuisance than the insects themselves. But what could one do among so many? He died at last, I believe, from over-devotion to his task, and his praiseworthy but ineffectual attempts to rid us of the pest came to an end.

Then we acquired a small black cat of uncertain heritage. It was only ever meant to be a pet, but within days of its arrival it declared war on our cockroaches; every conscious moment was spent hunting the abominable creatures and after six months the cat had done its work and the cockroaches were only very rarely seen and then not at all.

The cat is now the hero of our household and so far as I am concerned he is worth his weight in gold.

Venables, *Spectator*, 6 September 1900

Needling

My mother used to tell a story of an old cat, who used to sit on the table beside her mother's old housekeeper and play with her cotton-balls (reels were not in use in those days). It was a common custom to stick pins or needles in these cotton-balls if a pincushion was not at hand.

This cat, finding herself pricked by the needles when playing with these balls, used to draw them out first with her teeth in order to play with comfort.

If people would treat cats as they do dogs, and study them as much, they would be repaid by the amount of intelligence and sagacity shown.

Salf, *Spectator*, 7 February 1891

Foster Mother

FOR THE PAST six years at my house is Surrey, the blue tits have nested close by. For the first two years they built under an inverted flower-pot on a ground-floor window-sill, but the pot being transferred to another position, they followed it there.

We have often looked at them when sitting, and the bird has frequently remained on the nest while the pot was lifted and replaced. Once the greater part of the half-fledged brood fluttered off, and got scattered about, and had to be replaced through the hole in the top, seeming none the worse. Once away, they do not seem to return to the nest, as do the broods of the kind of wren, which builds a round ball of a nest in the bushes.

I unintentionally put the whole dozen or so of young birds out of one of these nests one Sunday morning, under a fierce fire of scolding from the old bird, found them all there again the following Sunday, and (finally, I imagine) put them all out again on the Sunday after that. Through all this time our cat watched with interest, chuntered vigorously when the birds were moved but never intervened to harm them. Indeed, she stayed often to guard them if I happened to be called away for a moment. Who is to say she did not feel a maternal interest, but then she was a rare cat who never killed birds or mice or other small creatures.

It may also interest your readers who care about this sort of subject, to hear of the singular incident at our farm two years ago, of a hen taking charge of three kittens.

The mother cat must have taken them herself an hour or two after their birth and placed them under the hen, which had made a nest for herself two or three yards off under the manger in a cowshed.

I saw the cat and her progeny lying on the straw directly after their birth, and noticed the hen on her nest. Returning an hour or two later, the cowman showed me the kittens under the hen, wondering how they had got there, as nobody else had been in the shed, and he had not touched them.

Till the kittens grew too big, the hen never left them; the cat used to go away foraging, and come down every now and then, throw herself down alongside the hen and nurse her young ones, sometimes lying with her head under, and her paws almost round, the hen's neck.

As the kittens got older, it was droll to see their foster-mother following them about and trying to cover them with her wings. For some six weeks it was quite the sight of the neighbourhood.

Newcastle Journal, 3 June 1893

Toing and Froing

W E H A V E two cats – the mother, Betsy, and her daughter Lina, two years old. When the kittens came, we had always kept one of each family, but we decided that the next that came should all be given away. Accordingly, when Lina's four kittens arrived, they were all sent away.

Three days later, Betsy had six kittens. On the cellar being opened in the morning where their bed was, Lina immediately took up the six kittens one by one to the attic, a distance of seventy stairs, doing it as quickly as possible, the last twelve being so steep that she had to hold her head very high to prevent her knocking the kitten she held in her mouth.

Having deposited them all in a box, she tried to take the mother, too, to the supposed place of safety. After four were taken away, she repeated this with the remaining two several times, nursing them as though they were her own in the box, not allowing the mother to keep them downstairs at all.

The mother then began to take the two kittens back but no sooner had she done so than the other cat took them back up the stairs and so it continued for hours until at last the real mother gave up and allowed the other cat to do her work for her.

Time and Tide, February 1840

A Tim of Gifts

EVERY ANIMAL seems more or less capable of affection, and those men and women who by kindness, sympathy, or some peculiar animal affinity imperceptible to human beings, but readily recognised by dumb creatures, have won the love of a cat, have wonderful tales to tell of his tenderness and devotion.

The most remarkable cat we have personally known was a grey tabby named Tim, who belonged to a family in Holloway. Tim's special peculiarity was his propensity for bringing gifts to his particular friends. Many people have been favoured with the present of a dead mouse now and again from their pet pussy; but Tim had a much keener perception of the sort of offering his human friends would like, and as he had no other way of obtaining what he wanted, he would steal from one person to give to another.

Two lady residents in his master's house won his special favour by their kind attentions and indulgences. Presumably his master's young daughter was not such a favourite with Tim, for on two occasions a small velvet-backed brush was mysteriously carried from her room and deposited in theirs, and once a pin-cushion was similarly conveyed.

It is possible that no one would have guessed that Tim was the author of these puzzling removals, but one day a strange noise was heard upon the stairs – a chinking and bumping sound. Someone went to see what it was, and lo! Timmy cautiously descending with his master's watch and chain in his mouth, the former knocking upon each successive stair as he came down.

The destined recipient of that choice gift, was, of course, never known. But Tim's most notable feat in the way of offerings of devotion did not involve a theft.

One day an escaped pigeon was seen sitting on the top of a tree in the garden next door but one to Timmy's home. All the cats in the neighbourhood were interested, but as the tree was fairly high, none of them had the courage to attempt to secure the bird. Tim was a fine cat in the prime of life, and possessed – as his master, who told me this tale, assured me – particularly powerful hind legs. He essayed to climb the tree, and successfully reached the top. He caught the pigeon dexterously in his mouth, and brought it down. Then he jumped the intervening walls and eventually laid the bird, alive and uninjured, at the feet of his master, who was watching the whole episode.

Another interesting London cat with whom I was well acquainted was Totsy, also a tabby. Totsy never did anything that could justly be called wonderful, but his general intelligence, and particularly what one may call his sensitiveness to human communications, and his peculiarly pretty 'manners', were very striking.

When he was outside a door and wanted to come in, we would hold quite a conversation with him. Like this:

Totsy: 'Me-ow!'

Friend: 'Do you want to come in?'

Totsy (in a tone of unmistakable satisfaction at being answered): 'Prrr-how!'

Friend: 'What, now, at once?'

Totsy (decidedly): 'Prohl.'

The door would be opened and Totsy, with a 'Prrrh' of thanks, in precisely the pleased and contented accents of a human being whose desires after some interval of suspense have been granted, would gently enter.

If, on the contrary, he was told from the inside to wait a bit, and not make a noise, he would keep quiet for some time, or relieve his feelings by whispered 'Me-ews', so soft as to be almost inaudible. He quite well knew how to modulate his voice, and speak softly when it was desirable. If he was in the room with us, and asking for some dainty, where he knew we could see him (also knowing that worrying at mealtimes was forbidden) he would open his mouth and go through all the appearance of mewing without making a sound.

Totsy was such a polite cat that if we spoke to him when he was sitting down, he would at once rise with a peculiar movement remarkably like a lady's graceful curtsey, and sit down again. He never failed to purr, 'Thank you', when a door was opened for him, and he would never jump on a chair or sofa, or on your lap uninvited, though he would sit up with his paws on the edge of a chair or couch and give you soft little pats to show what he wanted.

If he were scolded for a fault, that he knew to be a fault, he never resented it, but if, as happened on one or two occasions, he was spoken crossly to without a cause, out of mere ill-temper, he would retire in dudgeon, and not go near the offender again for the rest of the day, unless advances were made to him. This faculty for perceiving the difference between deserved and undeserved scolding was unmistakable in Totsy, and often astonished us.

One more instance of this dear pussy's keenness of perception I must give. I was one day doing some work with black, semi-transparent muslin. For fun, I put a piece over my face and looked at Totsy through it. I at once wished I hadn't, for the poor dear was so frightened at the sudden change in the familiar features that he fled

from the room in the greatest panic, and it was some time
before he dared to return.

Jennie Chappell, *Animals Worth Knowing*, S.W. Partridge, 1910

Playing Chicken

Kittens, especially if deprived of their natural protectors,
seem to long for the friendship of other beings, and will
often roam about till they find a person in whom they think
they may confide. Sometimes they make a curious choice.

A kitten born on the roof of an outhouse was by an
accident deprived of its mother and brethren. It evaded
all attempts to catch it, though food was put within its
reach. Just below where it lived, a brood of chickens were
constantly running about; and at length, growing weary
of solitude, it thought that it would like to have such lively
little playmates. So down it scrambled, and timidly crept
towards them. Finding that they were not likely to do it
harm, it lay down among them.

The chickens seemed to know that it was too young
to hurt them. It now followed them wherever they moved
to pick up their food. In a short time, a perfect understanding was established between the kitten and the
fowls, who appeared especially proud of their new friend.

The kitten, discovering this, assumed the post of
leader, and used to conduct them about the grounds,

amusing itself at their expense. Sometimes it would catch hold of their feet, as if going to bite them, when they would peck at it in return. At others it would hide behind a bush, and then springing out into their midst, purr and rub itself against their sides. One pullet was its especial favourite; it accompanied her every day to her nest under the boards of an outhouse, and would then lie down outside, as if to watch over her. When she returned to the other fowls, it would follow, setting up its tail, and purring at her. When other chickens were born, it transferred its interest to them, taking each fresh brood under its protection – the parent hen appearing in no way alarmed at having so unusual a nurse for her young ones. A curious incident of a cat's natural instinct being overridden by the need for some kind of social life!

Pall Mall Gazette, March 1898

Persis's Adventures

Persis was a dainty lady, pure Persian, blue and white, silky haired. When this story opens she was in middle age, the crisis of her life had passed. She had had kittens, she had seen them grow up, and as they grew she had

grown to hate them, with a hatred founded on jealousy
and love.

She was a cat of extreme sensibility, of passionate
temper, of a character attractive and lovable from its
very intensity. We had been forced to face Persis's difficulty with her kittens and make our choice – should we
let her go about with a sullen face to the world, green eyes
glooming wretchedly upon it, an intensity of wretched-
ness, jealousy and hate consuming her little cat's heart,
or would we follow Persis's wishes about the kittens, and
give them up, when they grew to be a burden on her mind
and heart? For while they were young, she loved them
much. She chose favourites among them, usually the one
most like herself, lavished a wealth of care, with anxiety in a small, troubled, motherly face, on their manners,
their appearance, their amusements.

I remember one pathetic scene on a rainy evening in
late summer, when the kittens of the time were playing
about the room, and Persis came in wet and draggled
with something in her mouth. We thought it was a dead
bird, and though regretting the fact, did not hinder her
when she deposited it before her favourite kitten, a shy,
grey creature, and retired to the lap of a forbearing friend
to make her toilet.

But while she was thus engaged we saw that the thing
she had brought in was a shivering little bird, a belated
fledgling, alive and unhurt. The grey kitten had not

touched it, but with paws tucked under him was regarding it with a cold, steady gaze. He was quite unmoved when we took it away and restored it to a profitless liberty, with a few scathing remarks on the cruelty of cats.

It is so nice and affectionate of a father to initiate his little son into the pleasures of sport and show him how to play a fish, but quite another thing for a brutal cat to show her kitten how to play with a live bird – a cat, indeed, from whom we should have expected a sympathetic imagination.

When Persis had washed and combed herself she came down to see how her son was enjoying his first attempt at sport; but no affectionate father sympathising with his boy for losing his fish would have been half as much distressed as Persis to find her kitten robbed of his game.

She ran round the room crying as she went, searched for the bird under chairs and tables, sprang on the knees of her friends to seek it, and wailed for the loss of her present to her son.

Again, there was no danger that she would not face in defence of her kittens. My brother had a wire-haired terrier of horrid reputation as a cat-killer. The name of the terrier, for an occult and complicated reason, was Two Timothy-Three-Ten, but it was generally abbreviated. Tim, large and formidable even to those who had not heard of his exploits, slipped into the room once where a placid domestic scene was in process.

Without a moment's pause the cat was on him like a wild beast. I caught Timothy and held him up, but the cat had dug her claws so firmly into his foot that she, too, was lifted off the ground.

As the kittens grew older, maternal tenderness and delights faded, maternal cares ceased, and a dull, jealous misery settled down over Persis. She had been left down in the country with a kitten once – alas! a tabby kitten – which was growing old enough to leave her when I came over for the day and went to see her. The kitten, unconscious of his unfortunate appearance, was as happy as most kittens; he walked round the cat and did not mind an occasional growl or cuff.

But she, not responding at all to my caresses, sat staring out before her with such black, immovable despair on her face that I shall not easily forget it.

Thus the cat's life was a series of violent changes of mood. While her kittens were young she was blissful with them, trustful to all human beings; as they grew older she became sullen, suspicious, and filled with jealous gloom. When they were gone she again became affectionate and gentle; she decked herself with faded graces, was busied with secret errands, and intent on aesthetic pleasure – the smell of fresh air, each particular scent of ivy leaves round the trunk of the cedar.

She caught influenza once in an interval of peace and came near dying, and, they said, received attention seriously and gratefully like a sick person; I was not surprised to hear that her friend sacrificed a pet bantam to tempt the returning appetite of the invalid.

While we were homeless for a year or more, Persis was lodged at the old home farm, and lorded it over the animals. Two cats were there: one the revered and hideous Tom, with whose white hair Persis had bestrewn a room in a fit of passion. He had left the house at once for the farm and wisely refused to return. Now he was a prop of the establishment. He killed the rats, he sat serene in the sun, was able to ignore the village dogs and cuff the boisterous collie puppies of the farm. So he met Persis on secure and dignified terms. It was well, for he had formed a tender attachment to her daughter; they drank milk out of a saucer together, looking like the Princess and the Ploughboy; and when the Ploughboy went out hunting (for he must vary his diet a little – unmitigated rat is monotonous) he invariably brought back the hind legs of the rabbit for the Princess.

Strange to say, the Princess was the only one of the grown-up kittens with whom Persis entered into terms of friendship; so while the Princess ate the rabbits of the Ploughboy, Persis ate the sparrows provided by the Princess, and they were all at peace.

She rejoined us again when we settled in a country town. The house was backed by a walled garden; exits and entrances were easier than in the larger houses where

Persis had lived with us before. She loved to get up by the wisteria, climb across the conservatory roof, and get in and out through bedroom windows. She found a black grandson cat already established, it is true, but in a strictly subordinate position.

Ra liked comfort, but his sensibilities were undeveloped. If he could get the food he desired (and he invariably entered the room with fish or pheasant) he did not care how or where it was given him; a plate of fish-bones in the conservatory would be more grateful than a stalled ox under his grandmother's eye, but to the old cat the attention was everything; she took the food not so much because she cared for it as because it was offered individually to her.

If Ra managed to establish himself on the arm of a chair he would remind the owner of his desires by the tap of a black paw, or by gently intercepting a fork. But Persis's sole desire was that she might be desired; the invitation was the great point, not the feast; she lay purring with soft, intelligent eyes, which grew hard and angry if the form of her dusky grandson appeared in the open door. She would get down from the lap on which she was lying, strike at the hand which tried to detain her, and – but by this time Ra had been removed and peace restored.

Her most blissful moments were when she could find her mistress in bed, and curl up beside her, pouring out a volume of soft sound; or when she was shown to company.

Then she walked with dainty steps and waving tail as in the old days, with something of the same grace, though not with the old beauty, trampling a visitor's dress with rhythmically moving paws, and the graciously modest air of one who confers an honour.

It came near to pathos to see her play the great lady and the petted kitten before the vet, who came to prescribe for her. Now she was all gratitude for attentions, and whereas when she was young she would not come to a call out of doors, but coquetted with us just beyond our reach, now she would come running in from the garden when I called her, loved to be taken up and lie with chin and paws resting on my shoulder, looking down from it like a child.

The old nurse carried her on one arm like a baby, and the cat stretched out paws on each side round her waist. She had more confidence in human dealings, too. I had to punish her once, to her great surprise. She ran a few steps and waited for me with such confidence that it was difficult to follow up the punishment, more especially as Taffy watched exultant, and came up smiling to insist on the fact that he was a good dog.

Taffy's relationship with the cat was anything but cordial. It was her fault, for he had well learnt the household maxim 'cats first and pleasure afterwards'. But Persis can hardly be said to have treated him like a lady; she did not actually show fight, but vented ill temper by pushing rudely in front of him with a disagreeable remark as she passed.

All this time Persis was growing old and small. Her coat was thick, but shorter than of old; her tail waved far less wealth of hair. She jumped into the fountain one day by mistake, and as she stood still with clinging hair under the double shock of the water and the laughter one noticed what a little shrunken cat she had become; only her face was young and vivid with conflicting passions.

Then the last change of her life came. We went to a place which was a paradise for cats, but a paradise ringed with death; a rambling Elizabethan house, where mice ran and rattled behind the panels; a garden with bushes to creep behind and strange country creatures stirring in the grass: barns which were a preserve for rats and mice; and finally the three most important elements of happiness, entire freedom, no smuts, and no grandson.

Persis was overwhelmed with pressure of affairs; one saw her crouching near the farm in early morning; met her later on the stairs carrying home game, and was greeted only by a quick look, as of one intent on business. The one drawback to this place was that it was surrounded by woods, carefully preserved. By this time, I had come to two clear resolves; the first, that I would never again develop the sensibilities of an animal beyond certain limits; for one creates claims that one has no power to satisfy. The feelings of a sensitive animal are beyond our control, and beyond its own also. And the second was this; since it is impossible to let an animal when it is old and ill live among human beings as it may when it is healthy; since it can by no possibility understand why sympathy is denied it and demonstrations of affection checked; I would myself, as soon as such signs of broken intercourse occurred, give Persis the lethal water.

I had been haunted by the pathos in the face of a dog who had been, and indeed still was, a family pet; but he was deaf. Even when he was fondled an indescribable depression hung about him; he had fallen into silence, he knew not how or why. Dogs respond to nothing more quickly than the tones of the human voice, but now no voice came through the stillness. Despairingly he put himself, as they told us, in the way of those who passed, lay on steps or in the doorways. Since we cannot find means to alleviate such sufferings we can at least end them.

But I never needed to put this determination into effect. The last time I saw Persis was once when she came to greet me at the door, and lifting her I noticed how light she was; and again I saw her coming downstairs on some business of her own, with an air at once furtive and arrogant, quaint in so small a creature.

Then Persis vanished.

She had been absent before for days at a time; had once disappeared for three weeks and returned thin and exhausted. So at first we did not trouble; then we called her in the garden, in the fields and the coverts, wrote to find out if she had returned to some old home, and offered a reward for her finding; but all was fruitless. I do not know now whether she had gone away as some creatures do, to die alone, for the signs of age were on her; or if she had met a speedy death at the hands of a gamekeeper while she was following up some wild romance of the woods.

So vanished secretly from life that strange, troubled little soul of a cat – a troubled soul, for it was not the animal loves and hates which were too much for her – these she had ample spirit and courage to endure, but she knew a jealous love for beings beyond her dim power of comprehension, a passionate desire for praise and admiration from creatures whom she did not understand, and these waked a strange conflict and turmoil in the vivid and limited nature, troubling her relations with her kind, filling her now with black despairs and painful passions, and now with serene, half-understood content.

Who shall say whether a creature like this can ever utterly perish? How shall we who know so little of their nature profess to know so much of their future?

Margaret Benson, The Soul of a Cat, 1901

Brahms and Liszt

MY CAT LOVES music. When I wind the gramophone and play Schubert she stares entranced. Mozart makes her purr profoundly. If it is Beethoven she arches her back and stalks around the player.

Brahms makes her spit. On hearing Liszt she leaves the room. If prevented she wails piteously until let out.

Robin Flowers, *Afternoon Outings*, 1883

Revenge!

CATS OFTEN show that they possess some of the vices as well as some of the virtues of human beings. The tomcat is frequently fierce, treacherous, and vindictive, and at no time can his humour be crossed with impunity.

Mrs A mentions several instances of this. A person she knew in a remote rural district had severely chastised his cat for some misdemeanour, when the creature immediately ran off and could not be found. Some days afterwards, as this person was going from home, what should he see in the centre of a narrow path between walls but his cat, with its back up, its eyeballs glaring, and a wicked expression in its countenance.

Expecting to frighten off the creature, he slashed at it with his handkerchief, when it sprang at him with a fierce hiss, and, seizing his hand in its mouth, held on so tightly that he was unable to beat it off. He hastened home, nearly fainting with the agony he endured, and not till the creature's body was cut from the head could the mangled hand be extricated.

A similar tale concerned a gentleman who had an only son, quite a little boy, who, being without playmates, was allowed to have a number of cats sleeping in his room. One day the father beat the boy for some offence, and when the father was asleep at night the cat attacked him, and might have badly injured him had not instant help been at hand.

Cats will often support their friends and attack perceived enemies of their friends in this way.

Pets and Other Animals, Williams & Booker, 1888

On Loan

Finally, I succumbed, went to a neighbour's where several superfluous kittens had arrived the night before, and begged one. It was a little black fellow, cold and half dead; but the Pretty Lady was beside herself with joy when I bestowed it upon her.

For two days she would not leave the box where I established their headquarters, and for months she refused to wean it, or to look upon it as less than absolutely perfect.

I may say that the Pretty Lady lived to be nine years old, and had, during that brief period, no less than ninety-three kittens, besides two adopted ones; but never did she bestow upon any of her own offspring that wealth of pride and affection which was showered upon black Bobbie.

When the first child of her adoption was two weeks old, I was ill one morning, and did not appear at breakfast. It had always been her custom to wait for my coming down in the morning, evidently considering it a not unimportant part of her duty to see me well launched for the day. Usually she sat at the head of the stairs and waited patiently until she heard me moving about. Sometimes she came in and sat on a chair at the head of my bed, or gently touched my face with her nose or paw.

Although she knew she was at liberty to sleep in my room, she seldom did so, except when she had an infant on her hands. At first she invariably kept him in a lower drawer of my bureau. When he was large enough, she removed him to the foot of the bed, where for a week or two her maternal solicitude and sociable habits of nocturnal conversation with her progeny interfered seriously with my night's rest.

If my friends used to notice a wild and haggard appearance of unrest about me at certain periods of the year, the reason stands here confessed. I was ill when black Bobbie was two weeks old. The Pretty Lady waited until breakfast was over, and as I did not appear, came up and jumped on the bed, where she manifested some curiosity as to my lack of active interest in the world's affairs.

'Now, pussy,' I said, putting out my hand and stroking her back, 'I'm sick this morning. When you were sick, I went and got you a kitten. Can't you get me one?' This was all. My sister came in then and spoke to me, and the Pretty Lady left us at once; but in less than two minutes she came back with her cherished kitten in her mouth. Depositing him in my neck, she stood and looked at me, as much as to say: 'There, you can take him awhile. He cured me and I won't be selfish; I will share him with you.'

I was ill for three days, and all that time the kitten was kept with me. When his mother wanted him, she kept him on the foot of the bed, where she nursed, and lapped, and scrubbed him until it seemed as if she must wear even his stolid nerves completely out. But whenever she felt like going out she brought him up and tucked him away in the hollow of my neck, with a little guttural noise that, interpreted, meant: 'There, now you take care of him awhile. I'm all tired out. Don't wake him up.'

But when the infant had dropped soundly asleep, she invariably came back and demanded him; and not only demanded, but dragged him forth from his lair by the nape of the neck, shrieking and protesting, to the foot of the bed again, where he was obliged to go through another course of scrubbing and vigorous maternal attentions that actually kept his fur from growing as fast as the coats of less devotedly cared-for kittens grow.

When I was well enough to leave my room, she transferred him to my lower bureau drawer, and then to a vantage point behind an old lounge. But she never doubted, apparently, that it was the loan of that kitten that rescued me from an untimely grave.

Margaret Benson, *The Soul of a Cat*, 1901

Military Marvel

FOR TWENTY-FIVE years, an oral addition to the written standing orders of the native guard at Government House near Poona, India, had been communicated regularly from one guard to another on relief, to the effect that any cat passing out of the front door after dark was to be regarded as His Excellency, the Governor, and to be saluted accordingly.

The meaning of this was that Sir Robert Grant, Governor of Bombay, had died there in 1838 and on the evening of the day of his death a cat was seen to leave the house by the front door and walk up and down a particular path, as it had been the Governor's habit to do after sunset.

A Hindu sentry had observed this, and he mentioned it to others of his faith, who made it a subject of superstitious conjecture, the result being that one of the priestly class explained the mystery of the dogma of the transmigration of the soul from one body to another, and interpreted the circumstance to mean that the spirit of the deceased Governor had entered into one of the house pets.

It was difficult to fix on a particular one, and it was therefore decided that every cat passing out of the main entrance after dark was to be treated with due respect and the proper honours. The decision was accepted without question by all the native attendants and others belonging to Government House. The whole guard, from sepoy to subadar, fully acquiesced to it, and an oral addition was made to the standing orders that the sentry at the front door present arms to any cat passing out there after dark.

General Gordon, 1867

Guests to Stay

Mrs F vouches for the following account, showing the hospitable disposition of cats. It was given to her by a clergyman, who had it direct from a friend. A gentleman in Australia had a pet cat to which he daily gave a plate of viands with his own hands.

The allowance was liberal, and there was always a remainder; but after some time the gentleman perceived that another cat came to share the repast. Finding that this occurred for several consecutive days, he increased the allowance. It was then found to be too much for two; there was again a residue for several days, when a third cat was brought in to share the feast.

Amused at this proceeding, the gentleman now began to experiment, and again increased the daily dole of food. A fourth guest now appeared; and he continued adding gradually to the allowance of viands, and found that the number of feline guests also progressively increased, until about thirty were assembled; after which no further additions took place, so that he concluded that all those who lived within visiting distance were included: indeed, the wonder was that so many could assemble, as the district he lived in was far from populous.

The stranger cats always decorously departed after dinner was over, leaving their hospitable entertainer, no doubt, with such grateful demonstrations as might be dictated by the feline code of etiquette.

Pets and Other Animals, Williams & Booker, 1888

Well Trained

SOME PEOPLE have an idea that cats can love places, but cannot love people. There can be no greater mistake. One of the young women employed in the refreshment room on the up-line platform, Great Western Railway station, Bath, has a tabby kitten of which she is very fond.

One Saturday, 15 June 1902, she went by an evening train to London, for a holiday, leaving the kitten in the charge of others. Her little pet saw her go. He waited until Monday quite patiently, and then, unable to stand her absence any longer, he made up his mind to seek her. He was seen to seat himself on the footboard of the 8.09 a.m. express to London, which stops at Swindon only, on the way to town.

The manageress of the refreshment room, too late to stop kitty, telegraphed to the station-master at Swindon, 'If kitten is found on footboard alive, return to Bath'.

The consequence was that the poor little traveller was prevented from going up to London to visit the queen of his affections, and arrived in a hamper the same morning at the Bath refreshment room. It is thirty miles to Swindon (sixty miles there and back) from Bath.

What loving thoughts little pussy must have had in his heart, to make him think of such a plan, and then sit so quietly on the footboard through all the whirl and rush, which must have sadly frightened him!

Dr Gordon Stables tells a similar tale of a pussy named Tabby, who was dearly fond of his mistress, a little girl. He would follow her wherever she went, and if parted from her, even for a few hours, seemed quite wretched.

W.H.G. Kingston, *Stories of Animal Sagacity*, 1874

Orange

THE TORPID CAT is really a kitten, but it is of enormous size, and a lively orange in colour. If it lies on the largest footstool it completely covers it, if it occupies an armchair it occupies the whole of it, if it honours the lap of a friend its head must be supported by one arm, while its tail hangs down on the other side, otherwise the centre of gravity could not be preserved and the torpid cat would slide slowly on to the floor and fall like a soft and heavy sofa cushion.

It has been lying on a green velvet armchair all afternoon; being temporarily displaced at tea time it fell asleep with its head on the fender; when the chair was relinquished it went back on to it, and it will lie there now till nightfall.

If you catch the torpid cat awake you will find that it has pleasant and intelligent hazel eyes, and a rose-coloured mouth carried half open to be ready for a yawn, as you carry a gun at half-cock waiting for a shot. If you stroke the torpid cat it stretches quietly, but not too far, for fear of waking up.

The ill-bred cat is a small mean English tabby, regularly marked. We made its acquaintance first when it was about six inches long and had come to take charge of the farm. It was sitting on a heap of coals cheerlessly surveying the prospect; when it saw us it sped towards us, crying loud

for sympathy and companionship. Then it spied Taffy and
went back to the fence to sharpen its claws.

The torpid cat, who was at that time a lively young
kitten, and the ill-bred cat made great friends. In the
evening the tabby kitten left the farm to take care of itself,
and came up to play with the yellow kitten. They played at
being tigers in a jungle. The tabby kitten hid between the
asparagus bed and the yew hedge; the yellow kitten sat by
the scullery door and pretended that he wasn't looking.
Then he began a swaggering walk towards the asparagus
bed; the walk quickened as he got nearer, until he was
suddenly clawed by the tabby kitten, and the shock of
surprise sent him flying into the air like a rocket.

Then in the twilight they fled about the garden,
crouched in the rough grass beyond the lawn, rushed
up the cherry tree and peered down, all with light, agile
movements, until as the light died you could hardly catch
the quick rippling of the tabby's stripes, and the yellow
coat of the other grew wan.

One morning the tabby came limping and crying from
the farm holding out a wounded, swollen paw. She was
taken into the house and doctored, but when the paw was
well she refused to go home. The two were inconven-
iently fond of human companionship – the yellow kitten
for its own sake, the tabby for a variety of reasons.

She grew more emphatically affectionate at meal times.
The yellow kitten used to accompany his mistress to feed

the hens; she thought he had an eye for young chickens, but found she slandered him. He was not looking at the chickens; his ear was open for the rustle of mice in the grass, and from time to time he dashed in and despatched one. He took special pleasure in doing this in company; it was always open to him to hunt in the garden, using his privilege when someone was taking the air and inhaling the breath of flowers. He seemed to think it added a point to evening meditation to hear the squeak of the dying shrew or to see the all-innocent fieldmouse untimely cut off while it was peacefully nibbling a blade of grass.

Just so both kittens, with the real self-consciousness of cats, played their games in public; they seemed to have no thought but of mock combat; then the scene of the combat shifted so as to be always in the eye of a spectator. The explanation is simple: the life of a cat is a continuous drama, ether actual or imagined; and what actor will play to an empty house?

The cat hunts not for food, but for sport, and the torpid cat, who refused yesterday to look at a mouse let out from the trap, spent the whole of this morning waiting behind the piano with his ear bent to listen to sundry little scratchings. The cat eats the mouse, it is true; and the sportsman eats venison, but he does not stalk for food.

'Animals,' says Mr Balfour, 'as a rule, trouble themselves little about anything unless they want either to eat it or to run away from it. Interest in and wonder at the works of nature and the doings of man are products of civilisation.'

But does this explain why the yellow kitten, as it followed me about the garden, spent some minutes in quarrelling with a pansy? The pansy lifted an inane, purple face towards the sky, and its head waggled helplessly on its stalk. The yellow kitten sat down beside it, and regarded it severely for a while. Then he slapped its silly face.

A change fell upon the kittens as they grew older. The root of the difficulty was that one had no ancestors at all, and the other only half the proper number. Their voices were too loud; their manners were bad. The yellow cat never mewed, but his purr was like a thrashing machine; the other was clamorous in pleasure and complaint, her appetite unquenchable, her demands for affection, for comfort, for food, insistent and unabashed.

She would try to drink from the milk jug while her saucer was being filled; she would run her claws into a hand to get firm hold while she ate the scraps offered her. If you put her out of the door she reappeared like a conjuring trick through the window; she would jump again and again on the lap of someone who did not want her; she would never take offence. One tithe of the rebuffs she met with would have sent a well-bred cat stalking with dignity from the room; the first of the refusals would have made him turn his back on the company and fall into deep and abstracted meditation.

But when her desire was accomplished and the hand weary of hurling her on to the floor, there was something disarming in the bliss on the little impudent face, as she nestled in utter confidence and licked the hand that had rebuffed her.

The yellow kitten was less pressing; just so much refinement of spirit as him refusing to stay in any place where he was forcibly put. He kept his muscles tense, like a coiled spring, and as soon as the grasp slackened quite slowly and deliberately he carried out his first intention.

The two began steadily to deteriorate. Now that the pressure of necessity was removed they were fast losing the stamina of the working cat; and having no sensibilities, natural or cultivated, luxury would never make them aristocratic; they had no education and little discipline, and they gave themselves up to revel in ungraceful comfort greedily and confidently demanded. Yet their affection for each other, their utter confidence in human nature, lends them a certain grace.

You may come into the drawing room and find the farm cat and the kitchen cat (for such are their real positions) settled in the best armchair. He is lying at luxurious length, sunk in deep slumber. Behind him, squeezed into a corner, sits the tabby; her anxious eyes peer out over his head, her soft little body is crushed by his weight, one tabby paw is round his orange neck. You rouse them and he half awakes; a long paw goes up to draw down the kitten's face to his own; and his rosy tongue comes out and licks her from nose to forehead, then he subsides again into slumber, and her eyes beam out blissful and honoured with the somewhat uncomfortable attention.

Or the little cat has been turned out of the dining-room because of her unceasing demands, and looks in forlornly through the window. Sandy awakes, sees her, gets on the windowsill and kisses her through the glass. Both kittens are entirely fearless with Taffy.

Sandy's is a mere absence of fear, greatly due to sleep, and Taffy may wag a tail in his face, just as a friend may flap a handkerchief in it, and yet only induce a flutter of an eyelid. The little cat, on the other hand, is a friend of his, will rub against his paws, and force him to take an ashamed interest in her.

But these are surface tendernesses; the position is fundamentally untenable. A cat must either have beauty and breeding, or it must have a profession. If it is well-bred it will take a hint; it cannot be disciplined, for a cat is a wild animal but its very aptness to take offence will bring to it a certain self-control; if it is a working cat it has its own profession, which occupies it very closely, it has its proper sphere and its own apartments. There is no help for it.

Kindly but firmly the tabby kitten must be induced to return to the farm: kindly, for the mistake is ours, we turned its head, we set it among temptations which its nature could not meet, and we gave it no early discipline.

Therefore, it must be led and not driven back. At this age, to coerce is to terrify; and there is something truly heartrending in looking at the shrinking, furtive air that punishments produce, and thinking of the happy, courageous little beast who sharpened its claws for an attack on Taffy, and gave itself up to the human being in blissful confidence of kind dealing.

Sandy is more of an enigma. One could tell his possibilities better if he would wake up. As he sleeps he grows larger and larger, though few have seen him eat, and he never asks for food. When a teaspoonful of cream is offered him his nose has to be buried in it before he can be roused to drink. He never scratches, he is never angry; when his hazel eyes open he looks with kindness on the company and falls to sleep again. There is only one time in the day when one can be sure of seeing him awake, and that is at prayers.

The presence of so many quiet people makes him feel it a good opportunity of amusing them by a little lively play with the bell-rope. If he is put out of the room he seeks an open door or window, and finds a chance of making a fine dramatic rush across the scene, accompanied by the stable cat. Prayers over, his vivacity subsides. He has a name waiting for him when he wakes, for Sandy is to be glorified into Alexander.

But what is the good of naming a cat who cannot hear you through his dreams? Sometimes I see visions of the future for the two. The first vision is peaceful and pro-saic: the tabby is instructing a rustic brood in the art of mouse-catching. She thinks no more of velvet armchairs, of porridge for breakfast and pheasant bones for lunch. Spruce and well-favoured, the very type of an English cat, guardian of the granary and terror of the mice, she licks her kittens' faces and brings them up to an honest, indus-trial career.

But there is something nightmare-like in the other vision: Alexander grown to panther size suddenly waking from sleep; his coat is a tigerish orange, his tail like a mag-nified fox's brush. What will he do? Is it torpor only that restrained the heavy paw from striking, and sleep that made the hazel eyes seem kindly? I find myself looking with a troubled wonder at Alexander as he fills the largest armchair. He is but eight months old – a kitten still.

Alas for Alexander of the pleasant hazel eyes; for he, too, has fallen a victim to the signors of the night. He was never known to poach, he never brought in a rabbit even, but it is spring, and pheasants are young, and keep-ers cruel.

So silently Alexander, too, has vanished away, and there is no redress.

Margaret Benson, *The Soul of a Cat*, 1901

Chapter Four

FIGHTING CATS

Hind Leg Hitters

OUT FOR A WALK one warm spring day I spotted two small creatures near the edge of a field. I thought they were hares and that impression appeared to be confirmed when the two animals stood on their hind legs and appeared to box with each other – exactly as mad March hares do.

Imagine my surprise then to discover as I drew a little closer that these two boxing hares were in fact cats – I watched quite spellbound as, for the next two or three minutes, their fight continued, almost all of it conducted while they stood and pranced backwards and forward, fists outstretched on their back legs only.

Ardvark, *Time and Tide*, February 1860

Bear Pit

A SWISS CAT lived in Berne. One day it was playing on the edge of a bear pit at the zoo, and amidst its frolics grew heedless, and fell between the bars down into the den. The spectators were dismayed, and thought to see it cruelly murdered; but no. The kitten was not frightened.

It bristled up as fiercely as possible in great wrath at the threats of Mr Bruin, and the great bear was regularly taken aback; it cowered, baffled by this tiny termagant, and instead of having its intended feast marched off, leaving the little cat to do as it liked.

The Clan of the Cats, Seeley, Jackson & Halliday, 1877

Gip, Gip, Hooray!

I KNOW A CAT myself, a cat named Gip, who is exceedingly fond of a great pug-dog that lives in the house with her; and I have seen these two lying before the fire, the cat right under Master Charlie's nose, forming a soft pillow for him; and I have heard that when they meet in the morning the two animals rush to each other, and each gives the other an affectionate greeting. And they take walks round the garden, and stop every now and then to kiss; and Gip is most jealous if Charlie takes much notice of anyone else.

I have read of a dog, too, also named Gip, who had two puppies; but after a time one died, and the other was given away. Just at the same time that Gip lost her pups in this way, a little stray kitten came to the house, and the poor dog took a fancy to it and adopted it. And so this dog and cat grew to be like mother and daughter.

It is an undoubted fact that cats often get fond of the dog that lives in the same house with them. One day a fierce bulldog had seized on a poor little terrier; he had got him by the throat, and though some men were trying to beat him off with sticks, they could not make him let go. Suddenly a cat, who was the terrier's friend, burst through the crowd, and fastened on to the bulldog's head and throat in such a furious way that she tore him terribly, and made him let the little terrier drop. It was half-killed; but, however, in time it got quite well.

The Clan of the Cats, Seeley, Jackson & Halliday, 1877

Hawkish

CATS OFTEN show great courage, especially in defence of their young. A cat had led her kittens out into the sunshine, and while they were frisking around her they were espied by a hawk soaring overhead.

Down pounced the bird of prey and seized one in his talons. Encumbered by the weight of the fat little creature, he was unable to rise again before the mother cat had discovered what had occurred.

With a bound she fiercely attacked the marauder, and compelled him to drop her kitten in order to defend himself. A regular combat now commenced, the hawk fighting with beak and talons, and rising occasionally on his wings. It seemed likely that he would thus gain the victory; still more when he struck his sharp beak into one of the cat's eyes, while he tore her ears into shreds with his talons. At length, however, she managed what had been from the first her aim – to break one of her adversary's wings.

She now sprang on him with renewed fury, and seizing him by the neck, quickly tore off his head. This done, regardless of her own sufferings, she began to lick the bleeding wounds of her kitten, and then, calling to its brothers and sisters, she carried it back to their secure home.

Arthur Buckland, *Animals I Have Known*, 1858

Life Saver (twice)

INSTANCES OF cats being the means of saving their owners' lives, by arousing them in case of fire, are of fairly common occurrence; stories are also occasionally told of a pet cat attacking a burglar and putting him to flight. But a little boy is living in Victoria, Australia, whose life has been twice saved by an intelligent cat.

On the first occasion, when he was less than a year and a half old, he was playing on the ground out of doors, and seized a large brown snake by the tail. The reptile was just about to strike the innocent babe, when the cat sprang upon it, caught it by the back of the neck and killed it.

A few months later the wee toddler wandered to a pond near his home and fell in. The mother missed him, and noticing that the cat stood at the edge of the pond, clawing the bank in evident distress, she rushed to the spot, just in time to save the little fellow, who was sinking in four feet of water.

Jennie Chappell, *Animals Worth Knowing*, S.W. Partridge, 1910

Crotchety

Picture to yourself a little girl, about two years of age, sitting on a low stool before a drawing-room fire. Coiled up on the rug is a favourite domestic cat. The child is in a fretful mood, and has been crying for some time. The cat endures the annoyance for some time, though evidently displeased. But even feline patience has its limits.

So pussy uncoiled herself, walked up to the child, and gave her a box on the ear with her closed paw, and then lay down again before the fire. The child, taken completely aback, cried louder than ever. Again pussy tried to endure it. Again her patience became exhausted, and she delivered a second box upon the ear, which nearly knocked the child off her stool. It was now the little girl's turn to be enraged. She rushed at the cat, and dragged it round the room by the tail. The mother I am delighted to say intervened on the cat's behalf and cat and child stared at each other malevolently for an hour or so before both went off to bed.

Time and Tide, 1899

Dog Fight

IT IS A COMMON thing for a cat with kittens to be ready to show fight to a dog, but Mistress Fluff, whose story is sent me by a friend who knew her well, seemed to possess even more than the average courage. The scene of her doughty deed was a grassy space in front of a crescent at Worthing.

Fluff had been brought out with her young family in a basket, by the girls of the family who owned her, for an airing in the sunshine, and fairly shook the basket with her loud purring as she lay curled up with her little ones playing around her.

Suddenly the peaceful group was disturbed by an invader. A terrier dog, the terror of all the cats, and the abomination of all the cat-owners in the neighbourhood, espied the interesting family, and bore down upon them.

But old Fluff was ready for him. With a fiendish expression on her face, her hair standing up on her back, and her tail like a brush, she gave a howl of rage and attacked the dog most heroically.

We thought poor Fluff was done for, for the dog was a noted cat-killer, and he had got her down and looked as if he was just going to shake the life out of her. At that moment one of the kittens gave a pitiful little cry. This seemed to put fresh courage into the mother cat. With one powerful spring she freed herself from the dog, and swearing furiously, leaped on top of the astonished enemy, and before we could do anything to help her, she had the terrier on his back, and was punishing him with tooth and claw.

When at last the dog escaped, he was covered with bites and scratches, and slunk home with his tail between his legs, utterly beaten for the first time in his life. And by a cat not half his own size, for Fluff was a small half-bred Persian, and the dog large for his kind.

Then Fluff, trembling with the effects of her supreme effort, but, strange to say, quite unhurt, returned to her

crying babies and soothed her own excitement by com-
forting and caressing them. The whole episode scarcely
lasted three minutes, but the terrier never forgot his lesson.
Whatever he might do to other cats, he kept a respectful
distance from Mistress Fluff from that day forward.

The Times, January 1892

Small but Deadly

An instance of the sagacity of a cat came under my own
notice. I was living, a few years ago, in a country place in
Hampshire, when one day a small tortoiseshell cat met
my children on the road, and followed them home. They,
of course, petted and stroked her, and showed their wish
to make her their friend. She was one of the smallest, and
yet the most active of full-grown cats I ever saw.

From the first she gave evidence of being of a wild
and predatory disposition, and made sad havoc among
the rabbits, squirrels, and birds. I have several times seen
her carry along a rabbit half as big as herself. Many would
exclaim that for so nefarious a deed she ought to have
been shot; but as she had tasted of my salt, taken refuge
under my roof, besides being the pet of my children, I
could not bring myself to order her destruction.

We had, about the time of her arrival, obtained a dog
to act as a watchman over the premises. She and he were

at first on fair terms – a sort of armed neutrality. In process of time, however, she became the mother of a litter of kittens; all but one disappeared. When she discovered the loss of her hopeful family, she wandered about in a melancholy way, evidently searching for them, till, encountering Carlo, it seemed suddenly to strike her that he had been the cause of her loss.

With back up, she approached, and flying at him with the greatest fury, attacked him till blood dropped from his nose, when, though ten times her size, he fully turned tail and fled.

Pussy and Carlo, after this, became friends; at least, they never interfered with each other. Pussy, however, to her cost, still continued her hunting expeditions. The rabbits had committed great depredations in the garden, and the gardener had procured two rabbit traps. One had been set at a considerable distance from the house, and fixed securely in the ground. One morning the nurse heard a plaintive mewing at the window of the day nursery on the ground floor. She opened it, and in crawled poor Pussy, dragging the heavy iron rabbit-trap, in the teeth of which her forefoot was caught.

I was called in, and assisted to release her. Her paw swelled, and for some time she could not move out of the basket in which she was placed before the fire. Though suffering intense pain, she must have perceived that the only way to release herself was to dig up the trap, and then

for whatever reason and he argued that if he kept that fox happy it would keep out other foxes that might be less scrupulous about the hen house.

'Nature abhors a vacuum,' he would say. 'If I kill her another fox will come in and if I kill him another one after that and I will be at it killing them forever. But she'll keep the others out and she's welcome so long as she does and she leaves my poults alone.'

The fox became semi-tame to the extent that one day the keeper saw from the kitchen window his fox playing in the yard with his cat. And once or twice a week from then on he saw the same old fox playing tag with his old cat. This continued for many months and then early one morning he saw the fox hovering thoughtfully close to the chicken house. It looked about as if to see if it was observed and then moved closer to the hens. Suddenly as if from nowhere the cat appeared and attacked the fox, spitting rearing and snarling all the while. The fox fled but a day or so later cat and fox were seen quite happily together, but well away from those chickens.

Countryman, February 1928

Jealous

I HAD A CAT which had long been an inmate of the house, and received all the attentions which it is well known old maids lavish on such animals.

Finding the mice were more than one cat could attend to, I secured a kitten, and wished to keep the two. My cat was indignant, and in very plain language requested the kitten to go.

I endeavoured to make peace, lifted both on to the table, and expostulated with puss. She listened with a sullen expression, and then suddenly gave a claw at the kitten's eye. I scolded and beat her, upon which she left the house and I never saw her again.

Dorothea Beale, *The Times*, 27 July 1895

Chapter Five

CAT VERSE

Jubilate Agno

For I will consider my Cat Jeoffry.

For he is the servant of the Living God, duly and daily
serving him.

For at the first glance of the glory of God in the East
he worships in his way.

For is this done by wreathing his body seven times
round with elegant quickness.

For then he leaps up to catch the musk, which is the
blessing of God upon his prayer.

For he rolls upon prank to work it in.

For having done duty and received blessing he begins
to consider himself.

For this he performs in ten degrees.

For first he looks upon his forepaws to see if they are clean.

For secondly he kicks up behind to clear away there.

For thirdly he works it upon stretch with the forepaws extended.

For fourthly he sharpens his paws by wood.

For fifthly he washes himself.

For sixthly he rolls upon wash.

For seventhly he fleas himself, that he may not be interrupted upon the beat.

For eighthly he rubs himself against a post.

For ninthly he looks up for his instructions.

For tenthly he goes in quest of food.

For having considered God and himself he will consider his neighbour.

For if he meets another cat he will kiss her in kindness.

For when he takes his prey he plays with it to give it a chance.

For one mouse in seven escapes by his dallying.

For when his day's work is done his business more properly begins.

For he keeps the Lord's watch in the night against the adversary.

For he counteracts the powers of darkness by his electrical skin and glaring eyes.

For he counteracts the Devil, who is death, by brisking
    about the life.
For in his morning orisons he loves the sun and the sun
    loves him.
For he is of the tribe of Tiger.

Christopher Smart (1722–71)

Epitaph for a Beloved Cat

BY YEARS and serious illness tired, I, poor gentle cat,
Am forced to face the infernal deep;
Proserpina smiling said to me,
'For you there will be now Elysian suns, Elysian groves.'
'But, if oh Queen of the night, this is to be my due,
To spend one last night with my dear master at his home
    before I depart forever,
I long to whisper in his ear,
"Puss still loves you though now gone forever beyond
    the Styx".'

Puss died in 1756. He lived 14 years, two months, four days.

John Jortin (1698–1770)

Ode on the Death of a Favourite Cat, Drowned in a Tub of Gold Fishes

'Twas on a lofty vase's side,
Where China's gayest art had dyed
The azure flowers that blow;
Demurest of the tabby kind,
The pensive Selima, reclined,
Gazed on the lake below.

Her conscious tail her joy declared;
The fair round face, the snowy beard,
The velvet of her paws,
Her coat, that with the tortoise vies,
Her ears of jet, and emerald eyes,
She saw; and purred applause.

Still had she gazed; but 'midst the tide
Two angel forms were seen to glide,
The genii of the stream;
Their scaly armour's Tyrian hue
Through richest purple to the view
Betrayed a golden gleam.

The hapless nymph with wonder saw;
A whisker first and then a claw,

With many an ardent wish,
She stretched in vain to reach the prize.
What female heart can gold despise?
What cat's averse to fish?

Presumptuous maid! with looks intent
Again she stretch'd, again she bent,
Nor knew the gulf between.
(Malignant Fate sat by, and smiled)
The slippery verge her feet beguiled,
She tumbled headlong in.

Eight times emerging from the flood
She mewed to every watery god,
Some speedy aid to send.
No dolphin came, no Nereid stirred;
Nor cruel Tom, nor Susan heard;
A favourite has no friend!

From hence, ye beauties, undeceived,
Know, one false step is ne'er retrieved,
And be with caution bold.
Not all that tempts your wandering eyes
And heedless hearts, is lawful prize;
Nor all that glisters, gold.

Thomas Gray (1716–71)

To Mrs Reynolds's Cat

CAT! WHO HAS pass'd thy grand climacteric,
How many mice and rats hast in thy days
Destroy'd? How many tit-bits stolen? Gaze
With those bright languid segments green, and prick
Those velvet ears – but prythee do not stick
Thy latent talons in me – and tell me all thy frays,
Of fish and mice, and rats and tender chick;
Nay, look not down, nor lick thy dainty wrists,
For all the wheezy asthma – and for all
Thy tail's tip is nick'd off – and though the fists
Of many a maid have given thee many a maul,
Still is thy fur as when the lists
In youth thou enter'dst on glass-bottled wall.

John Keats (1795–1821)

The Cat and the Moon

THE CAT WENT here and there
And the moon spun round like a top,
And the nearest kin of the moon,
The creeping cat, looked up.
Black Minnaloushe stared at the moon,
For, wander and wail as he would,

The pure cold light in the sky
Troubled his animal blood.
Minnaloushe runs in the grass
Lifting his delicate feet.
Do you dance, Minnaloushe, do you dance?
When two close kindred meet.
What better than call a dance?
Maybe the moon may learn,
Tired of that courtly fashion,
A new dance turn.
Minnaloushe creeps through the grass
From moonlit place to place,
The sacred moon overhead
Has taken a new phase.
Does Minnaloushe know that his pupils
Will pass from change to change,
And that from round to crescent,
From crescent to round they range?
Minnaloushe creeps through the grass
Alone, important and wise,
And lifts to the changing moon
His changing eyes.

W.B. Yeats (1865–1939)

On the Death of a Cat

Who shall tell the lady's grief
When her Cat was past relief?
Who shall number the hot tears
Shed o'er her, beloved for years?
Who shall say the dark dismay
Which her dying caused that day?

Come, ye Muses, one and all,
Come obedient to my call.
Come and mourn, with tuneful breath,
Each one for a separate death;
And while you in numbers sigh,
I will sing her elegy.

Of a noble race she came,
And Grimalkin was her name.
Young and old full many a mouse
Felt the prowess of her house:
Weak and strong full many a rat
Cowered beneath her crushing pat:
And the birds around the place
Shrank from her too close embrace.
But one night, reft of her strength,
She laid down and died at length:
Lay a kitten by her side,

In whose life the mother died.
Spare her line and lineage,
Guard her kitten's tender age,
And that kitten's name as wide
Shall be known as her's that died.

And whoever passes by
The poor grave where Puss doth lie,
Softly, softly let him tread,
Nor disturb her narrow bed.

Christina Rossetti (1830–94)

From: The Kitten and the Falling Leaves

THAT WAY LOOK, my Infant, lo!
What a pretty baby-show!
See the kitten on the wall,
Sporting with the leaves that fall,
Withered leaves–one–two–and three,
From the lofty elder-tree!
Through the calm and frosty air
Of this morning bright and fair,
Eddying round and round they sink
Softly, slowly: one might think,

From the motions that are made,
Every little leaf conveyed
Sylph or Faery hither tending,
To this lower world descending,
Each invisible and mute,
In his wavering parachute.
– But the Kitten, how she starts,
Crouches, stretches, paws, and darts!
First at one, and then its fellow
Just as light and just as yellow;
There are many now – now one –
Now they stop and there are none
What intenseness of desire
In her upward eye of fire!
With a tiger-leap half way
Now she meets the coming prey,
Lets it go as fast, and then
Has it in her power again:
Now she works with three or four,
Like an Indian conjurer;
Quick as he in feats of art,
Far beyond in joy of heart.
Were her antics played in the eye
Of a thousand standers-by,
Clapping hands with shout and stare,
What would little Tabby care
For the plaudits of the crowd?

Over happy to be proud,
Over wealthy in the treasure
Of her own exceeding pleasure!

William Wordsworth (1770–1850)

The Retired Cat

A POET'S CAT, sedate and grave
As poet well could wish to have,
Was much addicted to inquire
For nooks to which she might retire,
And where, secure as mouse in chink,
She might repose, or sit and think.
I know not where she caught the trick –
Nature perhaps herself had cast her
In such a mould,
Or else she learn'd it of her master.
Sometimes ascending, debonair,
An apple-tree or lofty pear,
Lodg'd with convenience in the fork,
She watch'd the gardener at his work;
Sometimes her ease and solace sought
In an old empty wat'ring-pot;
There, wanting nothing save a fan
To seem some nymph in her sedan,

Apparell'd in exactest sort,
And ready to be borne to court.

But love of change, it seems, has place
Not only in our wiser race;
Cats also feel, as well as we,
That passion's force, and so did she.
Her climbing, she began to find,
Expos'd her too much to the wind,
And the old utensil of tin
Was cold and comfortless within:
She therefore wish'd instead of those
Some place of more serene repose,
Where neither cold might come, nor air
Too rudely wanton with her hair,
And sought it in the likeliest mode
Within her master's snug abode.

A drawer, it chanc'd, at bottom lin'd
With linen of the softest kind,
With such as merchants introduce
From India, for the ladies' use –
A drawer impending o'er the rest,
Half-open in the topmost chest,
Of depth enough, and none to spare,
Invited her to slumber there;
Puss with delight beyond expression

Survey'd the scene, and took possession.
Recumbent at her ease ere long,
And lull'd by her own humdrum song,
She left the cares of life behind,
And slept as she would sleep her last,
When in came, housewifely inclin'd
The chambermaid, and shut it fast;
By no malignity impell'd,
But all unconscious whom it held.

Awaken'd by the shock, cried Puss,
'Was ever cat attended thus!
The open drawer was left, I see,
Merely to prove a nest for me.
For soon as I was well compos'd,
Then came the maid, and it was clos'd.
How smooth these kerchiefs, and how sweet!
Oh, what a delicate retreat!
I will resign myself to rest
Till Sol, declining in the west,
Shall call to supper, when, no doubt,
Susan will come and let me out.'

The evening came, the sun descended,
And puss remain'd still unattended.
The night roll'd tardily away
(With her indeed 'twas never day),

The sprightly morn her course renew'd,
The evening gray again ensued,
And puss came into mind no more
Than if entomb'd the day before.
With hunger pinch'd, and pinch'd for room,
She now presag'd approaching doom,
Nor slept a single wink, or purr'd,
Conscious of jeopardy incurr'd.

That night, by chance, the poet watching
Heard an inexplicable scratching;
His noble heart went pit-a-pat
And to himself he said, 'What's that?'
He drew the curtain at his side,
And forth he peep'd, but nothing spied;
Yet, by his ear directed, guess'd
Something imprison'd in the chest,
And, doubtful what, with prudent care
Resolv'd it should continue there.
At length a voice which well he knew,
A long and melancholy mew,
Saluting his poetic ears,
Consol'd him, and dispell'd his fears:
He left his bed, he trod the floor,
He 'gan in haste the drawers explore,
The lowest first, and without stop
The rest in order to the top;

For 'tis a truth well known to most,
That whatsoever thing is lost,
We seek it, ere it come to light,
In ev'ry cranny but the right.
Forth skipp'd the cat, not now replete
As erst with airy self-conceit,
Nor in her own fond apprehension
A theme for all the world's attention,
But modest, sober, cured of all
Her notions hyperbolical,
And wishing for a place of rest
Anything rather than a chest.
Then stepp'd the poet into bed,
With this reflection in his head:

MORAL
Beware of too sublime a sense
Of your own worth and consequence.
The man who dreams himself so great,
And his importance of such weight,
That all around in all that's done
Must move and act for him alone,
Will learn in school of tribulation
The folly of his expectation.

William Cowper (1731–1800)

CUTE CATS

Slide Rule

ONE WINTER OF heavy snow I watched a large black cat cross the grounds of our house every day. Then to my astonishment I watched as the cat climbed a six-foot high mound of snow that the gardener had shovelled up to clear the lawn.

At the top of the pile of snow the cat hesitated and then sat on the steepest slope she could find. Gravity did the rest and she slid down to the bottom of her mini ski run. I thought this must just – quite literally – be a slip, but no. The cat walked to the side of the snow mountain and climbed up again before launching herself once more on to her slope and shooting quickly to the bottom. She then did it again several times before wandering off with a very satisfied look on her face.

Surely this cat was tobogganing just for the fun of it?

J.F. Trevelyan, letter to The Times, January 1893

Presidential

DEAR KERMIT, we felt very melancholy after you and Ted left and the house seemed empty and lonely. But it was the greatest possible comfort to feel that you both really have enjoyed school and are both doing well there.

Tom Quartz is certainly the cunningest kitten I have ever seen. He is always playing pranks on Jack and I get very nervous lest Jack should grow too irritated.

The other evening, they were both in the library – Jack sleeping before the fire – Tom Quartz scampering about, an exceedingly playful little creature – which is about what he is. He would race across the floor, then jump upon the curtain or play with the tassel.

Suddenly he spied Jack and galloped up to him. Jack, looking exceedingly sullen and shame-faced, jumped out of the way and got upon the sofa and around the table, and Tom Quartz instantly jumped upon him again. Jack suddenly shifted to the other sofa, where Tom Quartz again went after him. Then Jack started for the door, while Tom made a rapid turn under the sofa and around the table and just as Jack reached the door leaped on his hindquarters. Jack bounded forward and away and the two went tandem out of the room – Jack not co-operating at all; and about five minutes afterwards Tom Quartz stalked solemnly back.

Another evening, the next Speaker of the House, Mr Cannon, an exceedingly solemn, elderly gentleman with chin whiskers, who certainly does not look to be of playful nature, came to call upon me. He is a great friend of mine, and we sat talking over what our policies for the session should be until about eleven o'clock and when he went away I accompanied him to the head of the stairs.

He had gone about halfway down when Tom Quartz strolled by, his tail erect and very fluffy. He spied Mr Cannon going down the stairs, jumped to the conclusion that he was a playmate escaping, and raced after him, suddenly grasping him by the leg the way he does Archie and Quentin when they play hide and seek with him; then loosening his hold he tore downstairs ahead of Mr Cannon, who eyed him with an iron calm and not one particle of surprise . . .

Letter to his son Kermit written by US President
Theodore Roosevelt, 1903

Cream Dream

I KNEW A BIG ginger cat that showed a considerable amount of sagacity in obtaining what she wanted. One day she found a cream jug on the breakfast table, full of cream. It was tall, and had a narrow mouth. She longed for the rich contents, but could not reach the cream even with her tongue; if she upset the jug, her theft would be discovered. At last she thought to herself, 'I may put in my paw, though I cannot get in my head, and some of that nice stuff will stick to it.'

She made the experiment, and found it answer. Licking her paw as often as she drew it out, she soon emptied the jug, so that when the family came down they had no cream for breakfast. A few drops on the tablecloth, however, showed how it had been stolen.

The taller cream jug was used on future mornings but the cat soon found a new way to get at the cream. She managed to balance on her back legs while placing both her front paws on either side of the brim of the jug. She leaned backwards until the cream spilled down her front and on to the tablecloth where she happily licked it up. Surely a case of intelligence?

E. Westall, letter to the *Spectator*, August 1870

Purr-fect Timing

A HIGHLY intelligent little cat of my acquaintance was also one of the most affectionate. Her young mistress used to go to school for a few hours daily in the neighbouring town. The cat would every morning sally forth with her, and bound along beside her pony as far as the gate, then going quietly back to the house.

Regularly, however, at the time the little girl was expected to return, the faithful cat might be seen watching about the door; and if her mistress were delayed longer than usual, would extend her walk to the gate, there awaiting her approach, and evincing her delight by joyful gambols as soon as she descried her coming along the road.

The cat would then hurry back to the house door, that she might give notice of her young mistress's return, and the moment she alighted would welcome her with purrings, cartwheels and caresses.

Arthur Buckland, Animals I Have Known, 1858

Forget-me-not

I WAS ONE DAY calling in Dorsetshire on a clever, kind old lady, who showed me a beautiful tabby cat, coiled up before the fire.

'Seventeen years ago,' said she, 'that cat's mother had a litter. They were all ordered to be drowned with the exception of one. The servant brought me one. It was a tortoiseshell. "No," I said, "that will always be looking dirty. I will choose another." So I put my hand into the basket, and drew forth this tabby. The tabby has loved me ever since. When she came to have a family, she disappeared; but the rain did not, for it came pouring down through the ceiling: and it was discovered that Dame Tabby had made a lying-in hospital for herself in the thatched roof of the house. The damage she did cost several pounds; so we asked a friend who had a good cook, fond of cats, to take care of Tabby the next time she gave signs of having a family, as we knew she would be well fed. We sent her in a basket completely covered up; and she was shut into a room, where she soon exhibited a progeny of young mewlings. More than the usual number survived, and it was thought that she would remain quietly where she was. Not so.

'On the first opportunity she made her escape, and down she came all the length of the village, and early in the morning I heard her mewing at my bedroom door to be let in. When I had stroked her back and spoken kindly to her, off she went to look after her nurslings. From that day, every morning she came regularly to see me, and would not go away till she had been spoken to and caressed. Having satisfied herself that I was alive and well, back she would go. She never failed to pay me that one visit in the morning, and never came twice in the day, till she had weaned her kittens; and that very day she came back, and nothing would induce her to go away again. I had not the heart to force her back.

'From that day to this she has always slept at the door of my room.'

Pall Mall Gazette, March 1888

Something Bruin

SOME TIME AGO, a machine of the cat species was received into our house under distressing circumstances, and adopted by our household. We have all rendered ourselves ridiculous in scientific eyes by becoming much attached to this rescued foundling, and he has assumed, under the name of Bruin, a position of importance which becomes his size, intelligence, and estimate of his own merits.

Under the second of these heads, I could furnish you with several interesting particulars; I content myself, however, with one, which relates to our machine of the cat species, and to another machine called a gas stove.

We had one of the latter articles put up in a study beyond the dining-room at the beginning of winter, and Bruin speedily selected it as his own particular place, in preference to the dining-room grate, no doubt because it was less frequented and the heat was more uniform. When the severe cold set in, it struck Bruin's master that it would be comfortable for him to have the stove to sleep by, and might tend to modify his erratic habits.

Accordingly, the stove was left alight (at half-strength), and Bruin signified his approbation by curling himself up in front of it early in the evening, and sleeping soundly until he was roused, under protest, and yawning widely, to a late breakfast, during all the nights and mornings which have since elapsed.

On Thursday night – Christmas Eve – his master left home, and it occurred to me to test Bruin's intelligence concerning that event. I left the stove unlighted, and watched his proceedings when the hour at which he usually retires to rest arrived.

He marched into the room with the air of important business to be immediately attended to which strongly characterises him, looked at the blank coppery space, uttered an angry cry, and ran out of the room to the coat-and-umbrella stand in the hall. He sniffed at a couple of waterproofs, but detected the absence of the familiar greatcoat and the sturdy umbrella which he associates with his master. Then he rushed upstairs, evidently with a strong sense of injury upon him, and I followed, to find him crying at the door of his master's bedroom, which I opened for him. He jumped on the bed, sniffed about the pillow, jumped down again, once more cried angrily, and ran downstairs.

I followed, and took my seat in the dining-room, pretending not to notice him. He sat for two or three minutes in front of the stove, then came into the dining-room and put his paws upon my knees, and gazed into my face with a gasp – not a cry, but a mode of speech which this machine has made us understand.

I pretended to be puzzled; he scratched my gown and gasped again. 'You are not thirsty, Bruin,' I remarked. 'What do you want? I am to get up, am I, and you will show me?'

I suited the action to the word, and he preceded me into the study, stepped inside the fender, put up his paws on the front of the stove, and turned his head towards me over his shoulder with a look of content that I had been clever enough to interpret his meaning, which gave me very sincere satisfaction. As I know that your readers are advocates for the study of animals otherwise than by the torture of them, I venture to send you this anecdote of an animal who really seems, to my ignorant mind, to have something like what we fancy we mean by 'consciousness'.

J. Rowe, letter to the *Spectator*, November 1860

Pigeon Fancier

YOUR READERS may be interested in a remarkable tale of a cat and a bird.

In a part of the loft a pigeon had built her nest; but her eggs and young having been frequently destroyed by rats, it seemed to occur to her that she should be in safer quarters near the cat.

Pussy, pleased with the confidence placed in her, invited the pigeon to remain near her, and a strong friendship was established between the two. They fed out of the same dish; and when Pussy was absent, the pigeon, in return for the protection afforded her against the rats, constituted herself the defender of the kittens – and on any person approaching nearer than she liked, she would fly out and attack them with beak and wings, in the hope of driving them away from her young charges. Frequently, too, after this, when neither the kittens nor her own brood required her care, and the cat went out about the garden or fields, the pigeon might be seen fluttering close by her, for the sake of her society.

Newcastle Journal, December 1864

Puppy Love

I HAVE A STORY to tell, of a cat which undertook the nursing of some puppies while she already had some kittens of her own.

It happened that her mistress possessed a valuable little black spaniel, which had a litter of five puppies. As these were too many for the spaniel to bring up, and the mistress was anxious to have them all preserved, it was proposed that they should be brought up by hand. The cook, to whom the proposal was made, suggested that this would be a difficult undertaking; but as the cat had lately kittened, some of the puppies might be given to her to bring up. Two of the kittens were accordingly taken away, and the same number of puppies substituted.

What Puss thought of the matter has not transpired, or whether even she discovered the trick that had been played her; but be that as it may, she immediately began to bestow the same care on the little changelings that she had done on her own offspring, and in a fortnight they were as forward and playful as kittens would have been, gambolling about, and barking lustily – while the three puppies nursed by their own mother were whining and rolling about in the most helpless fashion.

Puss had proved a better nurse than the little spaniel. She gave them her tail to play with, and kept them always in motion and amused, so that they ate meat, and were strong enough to be removed and to take care of themselves, long before their brothers and sisters. On their being taken away from her, their poor nurse showed her sorrow, and went prowling about the house, looking for them in every direction. At length she caught sight of the spaniel and the three remaining puppies. Instantly up went her back; her bristles stood erect, and her eyes glared fiercely at the little dog, which she supposed had carried off her young charges.

'Ho, ho! you vile thief, who have ventured to rob me of my young ones; I have found you at last!' she exclaimed – at least, she thought as much, if she did not say it. The spaniel barked defiance, answering: 'They are my own puppies; you know they are as unlike as possible to your little, tiresome, frisky mewlings.'

'I tell you I know them to be mine,' cried Puss, spitting and hissing. 'I mean to recover my own.' And before the spaniel knew what was going to happen, Puss sprang forward, seized one of the puppies, and carried it off to her own bed in another part of the premises.

Not content with this success, as soon as she had safely deposited the puppy in her home, she returned to the abode of the spaniel. This time she simply dashed forward, as if she had made up her mind what to do, knocked over the spaniel with her paw, seized another puppy in her mouth, and carrying it off, placed it alongside the first she had captured. She was now content.

Two puppies she had lost, two she had obtained. Whether or not she thought them the same which had been taken from her, it is difficult to say. At all events, she nursed the two latter with the same tender care as the first.

W.H.G. Kingston, *Stories of Animal Sagacity*, 1874

Hospitable

In the country town of Bradford-on-Avon there lives a little tabby puss, who is as good as she is pretty. It is her great pleasure to show charity towards cats in distress who have not so good a home as herself. One day she was seen to bring a lost, starving kitten to the back door, and to stand by looking pleased while he ate her own supper.

At another time she brought a black-and-white cat into the house, and not only shared her meal with the stranger, but also her comfortable armchair by the fire.

The mistress of this kind puss was surprised one night before going to bed to see two cats curled up on the chair instead of one, and she noticed that though the weather was then fine, a violent storm with drenching rain came on in the night.

Did her own puss, as many creatures can, feel that the storm was coming, and pity her homeless black-and-white friend, whose thoughtless people had gone off for a holiday and left her behind? It is sad to think that many people forget their poor pussies when they go away to enjoy themselves.

I think that the gentle, loving, puss who did her best for her little neighbour set a fine example.

Another young Tom cat in the same place seemed to feel the need of a brother, as he was the only puss saved out of a litter of five. He struck up a warm friendship with a poor little cat whose home was not so good as his own; brought him into the house, made him welcome at his own mealtimes, and invited him upstairs to share his master's bed, where he usually slept.

Edith Carrington, *True Stories About Animals*, 1905

Elephant Friend

IN THE GREAT Zoological Gardens [of Marseilles], we found specimens of all the animals the world produces.

The boon companion of the colossal elephant was a common cat! This cat had a fashion of climbing up the elephant's hind legs, and roosting on his back. She would sit up there, with her paws curved under her breast, and sleep in the sun half the afternoon.

It used to annoy the elephant at first and he would reach up and take her down, but she would go aft and climb up again. She persisted until she finally conquered the elephant's prejudices, and now they are inseparable friends. The cat plays about her comrade's forefeet or his trunk often, until dogs approach, and then she goes aloft out of danger. The elephant has annihilated several dogs lately, that pressed his companion too closely.

Mark Twain (1835–1910)

Maternal Mog

WE ONCE had a cat – a very epitome of maternity – and she would commit all sorts of petty depredations and give a peculiar kind of cry which never failed to summon the other cats, her housemates (not her own kittens) to share her booty, which she at once joyfully surrendered.

That poor little mother cat also, by accident, gave evidence that such as she can recognise form and semblance when artificially produced. She had brought up a kitten till it was old enough to be homed, and she had seemed to accept the parting with resignation.

About a week later, one of the young people brought home a cardboard kitten, one of those maintained in an upright position by a shaft behind it, after the manner of common photograph frames.

This had been stood upon the floor and left there, forgotten. The bereaved little mother cat, on entering the apartment, rushed towards the effigy with rapturous greeting. Then she stopped short, looked behind it, and raised her little face to ours with a wistful pathos that went to all our hearts, and the cardboard semblance was removed, and placed where she never saw it again.

She was a specially gentle, caressing animal, but absolutely fearless, and at any sound of dog or cat warfare in the garden, she would instantly rush out straight between the astonished combatants and stand there, striking an attitude of severe expostulation. Concerning the question of animals' ability to recognise the artificial representation of other animals the present writer, though never having had the opportunity of observing the effect of flat images on a creature's mind, has seen several instances of the unmistakable recognition of models.

Quite lately we have been making toy cats and dogs of swansdown calico, stuffed, and coloured as nearly as possible in imitation of nature. One of these, a miniature white-and-tan terrier, was introduced into a house where a cat was the great pet, and placed upon a shelf of a whatnot. Very soon, 'Bobs' discovered the arrival, and stood on his hind legs to investigate it. Next, a very care-ful paw was reached up by way of experiment. A claw caught the model, which of course came tumbling off the shelf.

Bobs, evidently under the impression that the stranger had flown at him, rushed away in terror, but soon came back under the fascination of the mystery. We put the toy on a sofa, to see what Bobs would do.

He came cautiously round, skirting the sides of the room to get a stealthy view of the intruder from behind. Then he ensconced himself on a chair, concealed by the head of the sofa, and took sly peeps round the corner at the object of his curiosity.

Finally, Bobs's mistress, fearing that he would ultimately seize and damage the model, put it out of his sight and reach. The model of a kitten produced a similar effect upon an Aberdeen terrier, who became frantically excited over it, and made an attempt to seize it every time he could get into the room where it was.

Jennie Chappell, *Animals Worth Knowing*, S.W. Partridge, 1910

Carriage Drive

THE AFFECTION of animals is usually a reward of kindness to them, but spontaneous and unsought attachments are not unknown. A black cat we knew at a country house, who was not an indoor pet, took an immense fancy to the master, although he did not care much for animals and had never noticed her. When he appeared in the stable yard she would follow him about like a dog, until, flattered by the attention, he grew quite fond of her. The creature's ambition appeared to be to go for a drive in the phaeton.

Time after time she jumped up when the gentleman and his daughter were about to start; but she was always discovered and sent down again, until one day she managed to conceal herself until the vehicle was on the road. She was then allowed to remain, and proudly rode on the front seat between them for about two miles. On passing under a railway arch, however, she became suddenly scared, jumped down and fled.

The young lady alighted also, to look for her, but the cat had disappeared, and they greatly feared that she was lost.

Nothing was seen of puss all that day; but next morning she was found, safe and sound, in her old place in the stable loft. In honour of this adventure the cat was taken into the house, and given the freedom of the dining-room hearthrug from that time forward.

Jennie Chappell, *Animals Worth Knowing*, S.W. Partridge, 1910

Cause and Effect

ONE OF THE strangest instances of a cat's understanding of cause and effect, and also her faculty for imitation, comes from the village of Mundesley-on-Sea in Norfolk, and we could scarcely have thought it credible, had we not the authority of an intimate friend who has been eye-witness of the performance. An elderly cat, named 'Midge', sole companion of an elderly widow, is in the habit, if the fire does not burn brightly enough to please her, of raking out the ashes from the lowest bar of the grate with her paw, as she has seen her mistress do with the poker!

Having produced the desired glow, she establishes herself in front of it, bolt upright, with her forepaws planted on the flat of the old-fashioned fender, and thoroughly warms her breast. So persistently does she do this, that her mistress dares not leave her alone with the fire unless the guard is on the bars.

She rakes very quickly, and presumably with outstretched claws, for she never seems to get her toes burned in the process.

Jennie Chappell, *Animals Worth Knowing*, S.W. Partridge, 1910

Stallion's Cat

IT WOULD SEEM that there is a tendency in the cat to form friendships with animals larger than itself, which friendships, like a cat's actions generally, appear to be spontaneous and self-originated.

The poet Oliver Goldsmith relates two stories of such attachments. In one case a black cat was so much attached to the celebrated stallion, the 'Godolphin Arabian', that when the horse died his little mourner sat upon the body until it was buried. She then crept reluctantly away, and was never seen again until her dead body was found in a hayloft.

In the other story the cat, when her horse friend was in the stable, never left her seat upon his back. The noble creature so appreciated the affection of his tiny friend that he would remain standing all night rather than risk throwing her off by lying down. (Or did he fear the sharp claws which she would naturally use to prevent herself sliding to the ground?)

Jennie Chappell, *Animals Worth Knowing*, S.W. Partridge, 1910

One-sided Passion

We knew a cat who lived in a house where strange dogs were frequently introduced, to remain until other homes could be found for them. To most of these dogs 'Altie' appeared quite indifferent, accepting them as they did her, as part of the ordering of the beneficent human providence that watched over them all, and therefore not to be quarrelled with. But one little dog was for a time an inmate of the house, with whom it was soon evident that Altie had quite fallen in love.

She followed him everywhere ('she' by convention, only, for Alfie was a fine Persian Tom) offering him attentions and caresses, even allowing him to share her food. The fact of this having so far occurred only once during the ten or twelve years of the cat's association with frequent canine strangers, numbering during that period, perhaps thirty or forty, shows how entirely the friendship was one of definite choice, but we believe it met with little or no response from the dog.

Jennie Chappell, *Animals Worth Knowing*, S.W. Partridge, 1910

Homing Instinct

THE HOMING instinct of the cat is well known, and many instances are related of cats finding their way over many miles of strange country in order to return to an old abode. But we think the following is one of the most remarkable.

'Many years ago,' says the writer, 'when residing at North End, Boston, I was possessor of a cat which my brother, who was master of a brig bound for Havana, prevailed on me to give to him, and just before sailing puss was taken on board the vessel then lying at one of the wharves not far away. Six weeks elapsed, when one day that cat appeared on our kitchen windowsill, and on being admitted gave many evidences of joy at being once again at home.

My first thought was that my brother had arrived with his brig, and puss, recognising old landmarks, had found her way back to us, but a diligent search along the wharves failed to discover any signs of the vessel, and it was not until several weeks had passed that I heard of her arrival in Portland, Maine.

Upon interviewing my brother with regard to the cat, he informed me that he had lost her while in Havana, and was much surprised to learn that she had reappeared in her old home. He eventually recollected that there was a Boston-bound vessel lying nearby, in which puss had probably taken passage.'

Jennie Chappell, *Animals Worth Knowing*, S.W. Partridge, 1910

It's for the Birds

TALKING OF honest cats, I must here tell a story which I have read, although I am afraid that some persons will find it hard to believe.

We all know how very fond cats are of getting hold of birds for their dinners. Well, Mr Wood tells us of one whose master and mistress kept a large cage full of doves. And one morning all the family were in a great fright because they discovered that Puss had actually slept in this cage.

Everyone thought that of course lots of the poor birds were eaten up, and would never coo to them anymore. But they made a great mistake, for when they came to count, all the doves were there, even to a nest of young ones, close to which Puss had slept – not one had been touched.

It was plain that, though Mrs Puss thought that all birds out-of-doors were wild, and quite common property, yet she understood that these belonged to somebody, and were not hers at all. Indeed, I think she must really have got fond of those birds, and learnt to love the little downy creatures. If not, it must have been hard indeed to keep from eating food of which she was so very fond. And though cats and birds do not generally love each other very much, or, at any rate, for very long, still such things have been known as cats walking about with parrots riding on their backs.

The Clan of the Cats, Seeley, Jackson & Halliday, 1877

Hospital Visitor

FOR MANY YEARS I considered cats a most awful nuisance and it is true they are serious destroyers of birds, but my views of our feline friends were changed utterly during a recent period when I found myself convalescing in hospital after a serious illness.

I asked for my window to be left open each day as the weather was warm, but lying in bed was tedious in the extreme.

One particularly bright morning I woke to find my window already open and a rather beautiful if small ginger cat seated on the windowsill and looking intently at me. We stared at each other for some time and then the cat gave a little meow and walked very delicately along the window ledge before hopping on to my bed.

At any other time, I might have shooed puss away, but I was intrigued and there was something about the way she looked at me that made me pause.

She walked carefully up the bed towards my head and something made me want o stroke her which I did. She purred loudly and settled down next to me for about half an hour. Then she left.

Next morning, I found myself dreaming that someone was applying a small rough file to my nose. I awoke to find the cat gently licking my face. I could not be angry and was secretly delighted she had returned for I have to admit that after she had left me the previous day I had missed her.

Now she was back. She stayed by me most of that day and if I spoke to her she meowed in reply or made a curious chirruping sound. Every day from then on she stayed with me and I'm certain she speeded my recovery.

When the car arrived for me on the day of my departure I thought I would never see her again, but as I waited on the steps of the hospital I saw something out of the corner of my eye. It was puss speeding towards me across the grounds. When she arrived at my feet she made a tremendous fuss and I asked the nurse if she was the hospital cat. 'She is a stray,' came the reply. There and then without a second thought I scooped her up and took her home, where we lived on the best of terms for the next ten years.

Robert Hooke, letter to The Times, July 1888

Dying for Love

A LADY IN FRANCE possessed a cat which exhibited great affection for her. She accompanied her everywhere, and when she sat down always lay at her feet. From no other hands than those of her mistress would she take food, nor would she allow anyone else to fondle her. The lady kept a number of tame birds; but the cat, though she would willingly have caught and eaten strange birds, never injured one of them.

At last the lady fell ill, when nothing could induce the cat to leave her chamber; and on her death, the attendants had to carry away the poor animal by force. The next morning, however, she was found in the room of death, creeping slowly about, and mewing piteously.

After the funeral, the faithful cat made her escape from the house, and was at length discovered stretched out lifeless above the grave of her mistress, having evidently died of a broken heart. The instances I have given – and I might give many more – prove the strong affection of which cats are capable, and show that they are well deserving of kind treatment. When we see them catch birds and mice, we must remember that it is their nature to do so, as in their wild state they have no other means of obtaining food.

Helen M. Winslow, Concerning Cats, 1900

Lucky Break

CATS HAVE A reputation for both good luck and bad. I would suggest that good luck and cats are firmer allies.

I was working in my laboratory one dark winter evening. I had tried an almost endless series of experiments adding this mixture to that, this chemical to that chemical without result. I would not say I was in despair for science moves in a very slow laborious way, but I had hoped for better progress. Then my pet cat Hodge, named after the great Samuel Johnson's cat, stepped gingerly into the room hopped on to the work surface to greet me and spoiled a jar of chemicals into a dish. The result for which I had been hoping appeared before my eyes.

A chance spillage had done the trick. I considered putting puss up for a professorship, but decided not to disturb her quiet life after all.

C.T.J. Wadham, letter to *The Times*, 1911

Mohammad's Cat

ALTHOUGH CATS have no place in the Bible, neither can their enemies who sing the praises of the dog, find much advantage there: for that most excellent animal is referred to in anything but a complimentary fashion: 'For without are dogs and sorcerers'.

The prophet Mohammad, however, knew a good cat when he saw it.

Muezza contributed her small share to the development of Islam for she sat curled up in her master's sleeve, and by her soft purring helped deepen his meditations. And did she not keep him dreaming so long that finally became exhausted herself, and fell asleep in his flowing sleeve whereupon did not Mohammad, rather than disturb her, and feeling that he must be about his business, cut off his sleeve rather than disturb the much loved Muezza?

Helen M. Winslow, *Concerning Cats*, 1900

Spirit of the Wild

Out of the basket there stepped a forlorn little figure, dusky grey, pathetically wailing, cold, hungry, and tired. He was not eight weeks old, every relation and friend in the world was left far behind him; but he was in entire possession of himself and his manners. The ruffled coat was a uniform tint; the little pointed head gave evidence of the long pedigree he trailed behind him. In these weary and destitute circumstances, the true air of noblesse oblige was on him.

His very appetite had deserted him, and for days he had to be forcibly fed with warm milk in a teaspoon. He remonstrated about this, but it impaired not the least his confidence in human nature.

Then he grew better, and became an elf-like creature, playing rather seriously with his own tail, but venturing not far from the skirts of his mistress. Once he saw the old cat, and would have run to her, but she turned on him a look so malevolent that we snatched him out of harm's way, and still scowling she proceeded to take possession of his sleeping basket. She used it for a day or two, but finding that it had been given up to her she abandoned it.

When I joined Mentu and his mistress on a tour in Cornwall some weeks later he had become a different creature. He was still very polite, but had grown in size and in confidence, and he was fast developing the drama of the cat and the madness of the kitten's spirits. He whirled round the room to catch the crackling paper hanging on a string; he played the clown with a cardboard paper-basket, hurling himself into it with such force that it upset and poured him out like water on the other side; he retrieved paper balls, and hanging over the bars of chairs and tables beat them with the tips of his paws; he hid them under corners of carpets and expended an immense amount of time and strategy in finding them again. The paper flew into the air, and sped across the room so fast that only a very clever and agile kitten could ever have caught it. Then Mentu discovered the Shadow Dance.

One evening while the paper was swinging on a string in the lamplight, Mentu suddenly saw the shadow. Thenceforward he renounced the substance and deliberately pursued the shadow. If the actual paper came in his way he hit it with a pettish gesture, and searched the carpet for the shadow. And he knew the two were connected, for at sight of the paper he began to look about for the shadow. Then he rushed after it, and through it; he spread himself out on the carpet to catch it, and it was gone; he fled round and round in a circle after it, and cared for nothing so much as the pursuit of nothingness.

We went to an empty hotel, hidden in a little bay near the Lizard. Green slopes, covered even in March with flowering gorse, fall quickly to the pillared basalt coves. Here you may sit on slabs of rock sheltered from east and north wind, scenting the sweet, pungent incense breath of the gorse, and watching the gulls at play beneath. You can see the great liners pass, signalling at Lloyd's station, and branching off below the Lizard Lights to cross the ocean; or you can watch the gallant ships come in, corn laden, with men crowding to the side for their first glimpse of English shores.

But, except on Sunday, when Lizard Town walks two and two on the cliff, you see no man there and hardly a stray beast. So here Mentu became the companion of our strolls, scudding across open stretches of green, rushing into shelter from imagined foes under gorse and heather, dancing with sidelong steps and waving tail down little grassy slopes, or lying on ledges of rock as grey as himself, starred with lichen as yellow as his eyes.

Once we went out along the cliff to return by the road, but here Mentu's faith in us deserted him. He set out to go home alone, but dared not; he wished to come with us, but was tired; he would not be carried for he saw children in the distance, and a cat prefers to trust its own sense and agility in danger. So in despair of his wavering decision we walked on, until, turning, we caught sight of a pathetic figure silhouetted against the dusty road – a silky kitten with wide mouth opened in a despairing outcry against fate.

Once Mentu met a cow grazing on the cliff. Here was terror, but that he realised the compelling power of the feline eye. He fixed on her two yellow orbs with fear-distended pupils, prepared to make himself very large and terrible by an arched back if she so much as turned towards him, and thus holding her paralysed with terror (though she appeared to graze unconcernedly the while) he walked by with tiptoe dignity and scudded to shelter.

But Mentu himself was once nearly petrified by a very awful kind of Gorgon. He was tripping and smelling, and coming to the edge of a little stone well he looked in. Suddenly we saw him turn rigid, with a face of inexpressible horror. He stood statue-like for a moment, then lifting silent paws retired backwards noiselessly, imperceptibly, step by step from the edge. Once out of sight of the pool he turned and fled. I went to look in. A frog sat there.

Sometimes we went down a stony winding path to the cove beneath; a wren was building here, for the cock-wren sat on a bush and girded at Mentu as he passed. One day I heard from far below the sharp note whirring like a tiny watchman's rattle, and returned to find Mentu lying on the path with swishing tail cruelly eyeing the atom which scolded him from above.

When the time came to go home Mentu had undergone another transformation. He had trebled in size; he had lost the rough, reddish 'kitten hair'; his coat was shining, silky, ashen-grey; his eyes were the colour of hock.

Blue Persians were not plentiful in Cornwall, and a little crowd followed us up and down the platform, for Mentu travelled no longer in a basket. In the train he was perfectly calm; looked out of the window at stations, and regarded railway officials with an impartial and critical eye. A fellow traveller pronounced him 'a kind of dog-cat', alluding, we supposed, to his intelligent and self-possessed demeanour as he sat upright on his mistress's lap.

We parted again, and from time to time I had accounts of Mentu. In spring time he relinquished the pursuits of shadows in favour of less innocuous sport. He was found curled up in a blackbird's nest, meditating on the capital dinner he had made of the inhabitants. He laid little offerings of dead, unfledged birds on his mistress's chair or footstool. He was seen trotting across the lawn, his head thrown proudly back, so that the nest he was bringing her should clear the ground. Saddest of all, she hung up a cocoanut for the tits outside her window, and a dead blue tit was soon laid at her feet.

Again, it was said that he appeared suddenly, like the Cheshire cat, on a tree, miles from home; and in early autumn, in the morning, he was seen crossing the lawn with a train of seventeen angry pheasants behind him.

We renewed acquaintance when I came to stay at Mentu's home. He was out when I arrived, and as we sat with open windows in the growing dusk there was a sudden soft leap, and a presence on the window – a wild creature, with shining eyes, the very incarnation of the dusk. Even as he jumped down and came to our feet the mood changed. He purred to us, and went to his dinner plate. Finding there a satisfactory mess he began to eat, turning round to throw rapid, grateful glances towards his mistress, purring the while.

Like the Dean who gave thanks for an excellent dinner, or a moderately good dinner, so Mentu is wont to graduate his grace according to his meat. A fish's head, or the bones of a partridge (it was long before his mistress could be persuaded that he would not prefer a nicely filleted sole) will produce the most grateful glances and the loudest purrs.

As I was occupying the sofa, Mentu took his after-dinner nap on my feet. It is odd that cats show an intense dislike to anything destined and set apart for them. Mentu has a basket of his own, and a cushion made by a fond mistress, but to put him into it is to make him bound out like an India-rubber ball. He likes to occupy proper chairs and sofas, or even proper hearthrugs. In the same way, the well-bred cat has an inconvenient but aesthetic preference for eating its food in pleasant places, even as we consume chilly tea and dusty bread and butter in a summer glade. A plate is distasteful to a cat, a newspaper still worse; they like to eat sticky pieces of meat sitting on a cushioned chair or a nice Persian rug. Yet if these were dedicated to this use they would remove elsewhere. Hence the controversy is interminable.

The next few days Mentu was determined to devote to family life. He came to the drawing-room in the evening and was very affable and polite. He went readily to anyone who invited him, and dug his claws encouragingly into their best evening dresses. We had taught him a trick in Cornwall which he still remembered. He lies on his back, two hands are put under him, and he is gently raised. A touch on elbows and knees makes him shoot forelegs and hind legs outwards and downwards; so that head and forelegs hang down at one end, hind legs and tail at the other, and the great grey cat lies curved into crescent shape, purring serenely.

In the course of the evening my collie, a visitor with me, came genially into the room. Mentu did not know him; he sat upright, with eyes fixed upon the dog, shaking with terror, but making no attempt to escape. I heard Mentu calling on his mistress early next morning in a querulous tone. As her door was shut I invited him into my room, but he found it not to his mind, and soon left me. He sat all the morning with us, but was easily bored, and walked about uttering short bored cries until he could find someone to play with him. He delighted in a game of hide and seek, which he had instituted for himself. He hid and called out, lay still till he was seen, and then sprang up to scud across the room.

When we went into the garden he followed, and the scolding of a blackbird made us look up to see him on a branch overhead staring down at us. He walked with us, too, or rather when we walked he plunged rustling through the bushes bordering the path, and flashed out to stand a moment in the open. Withal one felt that a thinking being moved with us, whether bored or childishly excited, gently affectionate or suddenly grateful; a being thoroughly self-conscious, greedy of admiration, regarding himself and us, and taking his life into his own hands.

And close beneath the surface of his civilisation lay the wild beast mature. One could wake it in an instant, for if I caught his eye the surface flashed sapphire for a moment, then the eye with distended pupils was fixed upon me, and silently, holding me by the eye, he believed, he stole across the room, and jumped up suddenly almost in my face. There was something uncanny about it, and even possibly dangerous, for if I looked up from a book sometimes I found that topaz eye trying to catch and arrest my own, while the great cat stole silently nearer.

I think if we had not relinquished the game Mentu's claws would have blinded me. For the wild nature in Mentu is as strong as his inbred civilisation; and the two are at strife together. His heart and his appetite lead him back and back to the house; keep him there for days together – a dainty fine gentleman, warm-hearted, capricious. But the spirit of the wild creature rises in him, and the night comes when at bedtime no Mentu is to be found.

Margaret Benson, *The Soul of a Cat*, 1901

Hare Today

A MAN GOING through a hayfield once saw a cat and a hare at play quite prettily together.

One would think that this cat must have heard of a hare called Puss, as the poet Cowper called his pet hare, and so got to think that hares were near relations of hers.

The hare even followed its new friend almost to the farm gate before realising its mistake and scampering off. The cat looked quite disconsolate to see its friend vanish into the distance.

The Times, December 1905

Cupboard Love

M R WENZEL'S CAT was so exceedingly fond of a particular dog that she was always with him; and I suppose he must have been as fond of her, or he would have barked, and driven her away.

They used to lie and sleep together by the same fire, or on the same rug at night; they ate of the same food, and out of the same saucer; and when they went out for a walk it was always together. Mr Wenzel was very much amused at them; and he thought that he would try the cat's friendship a bit; and so this is what he did.

One day he took the cat into the dining-room, but kept the dog out. He had his own dinner and gave Puss a good share. He was eating partridge, and Puss found it very delicious, and most beautifully tender.

She seemed to enjoy herself very much, and Mr Wenzel fancied that she was not thinking of her friend at all. When he had done, his wife put half a partridge away in a cupboard, placing a cover over it. She pushed the door to, but did not quite shut it. Very soon the door of the room was opened and Mr Wenzel went out, and the cat too.

She rushed off to find her dear friend, and soon came back with him into the dining-room, and going straight to the cupboard she pulled the door open, pushed off the cover, and showed the grand feast to the dog, who was greatly delighted, and very soon ate it all up.

The Clan of the Cats, Seeley, Jackson & Halliday, 1877

Swiss Please

DURING SIX WEEKS which I spent at the Diablerets, in Switzerland, several years ago, I had the pleasure of making acquaintance with a very remarkable cat.

His mistress, a very clever and interesting lady, nearly related to a celebrated Independent divine, brought him with her to the hotel, and opened his basket in her room.

This done, puss looked about him, reconnoitred the locality, and then walked out leisurely, to spend his day in the adjacent fields and woods, returning at night to his bed and supper in his mistress's room.

Miss L assured me that she had carried the cat all over the Continent with her, and that this was his invariable practice.

Perhaps if this letter should fall under her notice, she will favour us with further details respecting her intelligent *compagnon de voyage*. Certainly I saw enough with my own eyes to realise that this cat had some sense, some consciousness, of what it was doing and where it was going as it travelled often, not in a box or basket, but by its mistress's side, almost one might say like a human companion. Perhaps we must recognise the neglected truth that both the moral and the intellectual qualities of the higher animals vary in individuals between the poles of something like heroism and baseness, genius and idiocy. The Swiss cat was perhaps an example of genius?

Philozooist, *Spectator*, 27 August 1881

Musical Tom

I KNEW A CAT, many years ago – a black Tom – rather heavy and dull in his ways, for the most part, but with two qualities very strongly marked – love for music and affectionateness.

He knew good music from bad, perfectly well, would sit on the step of a piano with great content and purring, so long as a capable performer was playing, and if the execution were very good indeed, would testify his delight by arching his tail, walking across the keys, and sitting down in the performer's lap.

On the other hand, bad playing always drove him away; and I remember there was one member of the family whose performance always sent him off in disgust.

So much for the artistic side of his temperament. Now for the affections.

His mother was always very fond of her kittens, and used to sit over them very closely during the first early weeks of their lives, too closely, her son thought, after he grew old enough to consider about things.

I have more than once seen him go up to her, as she nestled over the young ones in the basket, and apparently whisper something; whereupon she would get out, stretch herself and go into the garden for a little fresh air while he got in to her place and lay over the kittens to keep them warm till she came back when he resigned his charge to her again. I regret to say that he died, still a comparatively young cat, of distemper.

Richard Littledale, *Time and Tide*, 3 September 1881

Home Loving

I<small>N</small> <small>THIS</small> <small>CITY</small> there is a large hospital set up as a temporary measure but slowly being made permanent. As the new buildings go up, the occupiers of one ward remove to the other end of the place, to a ward precisely similar, and in every respect as comfortable as the one they left, but built of brick and stone rather than timber.

'Tabby', from its birth, had been a cherished inmate of one of the old wards, and had gone in and out as a kind of privileged mistress for four or five years, and had been an object of constant attention and affection from both nurses, especially from the younger woman of the two, which affection was duly and well returned by Tabby.

But on the removal of the nurses to the other ward, Tabby refused to go with them. She allowed herself to be carried over, but to the chagrin and mortification of her friends, she returned to her old abode.

On hearing these facts, I went over and saw her hanging about her old dwelling. Even when the timber structure was entirely demolished, Tabby climbed the pile of rotting timbers and sat there as if defying the world to take away the last vestige of her old home. This incident of feline experiences is set down without note or comment.

E.H., *Spectator*, 3 September 1867

On the Dot

SHE WAS handsome as to size; her coat was a beautiful, glossy black, and at the throat was a pretty, white star. Each day, as the different articles of food were brought in for dinner and placed on the table, the charge always was, 'Now, Dot, come here and take care of this till I come back.'

Dot mounted guard at once, on a chair at the side of the table, and was never known to leave her post till the viands were claimed. Whether it was beef, mutton, fish or game, all was perfectly safe; and she was quite contented when a cooked morsel after dinner was given to her as a reward. Her own dinner, though placed close beside her, she never touched, but always waited till it was given to her, however hungry she was known to be.

She was obedient to all orders, one of which was that she was not to come to my room. I prefer to keep at a respectful distance from even domestic pets however excellent their individual characters.

But one very cold evening of a very severe winter, Dot, passing all the other rooms, to which she had perfect freedom, came to my door, and with a special petition, to which my attention was drawn, as being something quite unusual in cat language, waited till she was told she might come in.

The good creature placed herself before the bright fire, and purred, to her and our great pleasure – a self-invited and truly happy guest. She never once encroached on this one little special favour.

M.D., *Spectator*, September 1870

Hunting Pair

IN THE BACK-KITCHEN premises of an old manor house, amongst hampers, and such like odds and ends, a cat had a litter of kittens. They were all removed but one, and as the mother was frequently absent, a hen began laying in a hamper close by.

For a time, all things went well, the hen sitting on her eggs and the cat nursing the kitten within a few inches of each other. The brood were hatched out, and almost at the same time the old cat disappeared.

The chickens were allowed to run about on the floor for sake of the warmth from a neighbouring chimney, and the kitten was fed with a saucer of milk in the same place, both feeding together frequently out of the same dish. The hen used to try to induce the kitten to eat meal like the chicks, calling to it and depositing pieces under its nose in the most amusing way, finally doing all in its power to induce the kitten to come, like her chicks, under her wings.

The result was nothing but a series of squalls from the kitten, which led to its being promoted from the back to the front kitchen, where it was reared until it was grown up.

At this time a young terrier was introduced into the circle, and after many back-risings and bad language on pussy's part, they settled down amicably and romped about the floor in fine style. Eventually the terrier became an inveterate rabbit-poacher – killing young rabbits and bringing them home – a proceeding to which the cat gave an intelligent curiosity, then a passive and purring approval, and finally, her own instincts having asserted themselves, she went off with the dog hunting in the woods.

Our own keeper reported them as getting 'simply owdacious', being found a great distance from the house; and keepers of adjacent places also said the pair were constantly seen hunting hedgerows on their beats.

On one occasion I saw them myself hunting a short hedge down systematically, the dog on one side, the cat on the other; and on coming near an open gateway, a hare was put out of her form, and bounding through the open gate was soon off; the dog followed, till he came through the gateway, where he stood looking after the hare; and the cat joining him, they apparently decided it was too big or too fast to be successfully chased, so resumed the hedge hunting, each taking its own side as before. They frequently returned home covered with mud, and pussy's claws with fur, and would lie together in front of the fire, the cat often grooming down the dog, licking him and rubbing him dry, and the dog getting up and turning over the ungroomed side to be finished.

This curious friendship went on for six months or more, till the dog had to be kept inside to save him from traps and destruction. The cat, nothing daunted, went on with her poaching until one day she met her fate in a trap, and so their partnerships came to an end.

The dog was a well-grown fox-terrier, and the cat a tabby of nothing beyond ordinary characteristics, save in her early life having been fostered by a hen, and in her prime the staunch friend and comrade of poor old 'Foxie'.

If there are 'happy hunting grounds' for animals hereafter, and such things are allowed them, no doubt they will renew their intimacy, and their poaching forays, together there.

Graham Simmonds, *Spectator*, 8 April 1895

Missing the Master

It seems to me that the great independence of mind shown by even the most domesticated of cats is evidence of a strength of character quite unusual among animals.

Of all pets, they give the least trouble; they forage for themselves largely, wash themselves, take exercise of their own accord; less dependent on man than a dog, they are yet capable of strong attachments.

My cat, a Persian, is warmly attached to me; even if asleep on anyone else's lap, the moment I speak or call her, she runs to me. Whenever she catches a mouse or finds herself some dainty, it is at once brought to me and laid at my feet with a special cry – never used at any other time.

When I was ill in the winter and confined to bed for some weeks, pussy was with me day and night, only leaving me for half an hour at dinner-time. Efforts were made to coax her into other rooms equally warm and comfortable, for other invalids were in the house, but nothing would induce her to leave me; and when at last I went abroad for some weeks, I returned to find the poor cat at death's door. She had scarcely eaten, was unkempt, and had refused, after one vain search, ever to come upstairs, even to the dining-room floor, and this though every attention had been bestowed on her.

I have noticed a curious thing when she has kittens – that she graduates the size of the mice she brings them, half-stunning the mice first; but even so, the kittens appear terribly afraid of their new plaything, and for some time dare not take part in the game.

Is the taste for mice a cultivated one? The taste for fish must surely be, since cats could never have caught them for themselves; their fondness for shellfish is especially puzzling, as they are quite unable to get at the meat without aid. Have we here a clear case of inherited instincts?

One more question. Has anyone ever attempted to breed a special race of cats, for special characteristics, as has been done with dogs? If not, is it fair to compare the intelligence of one with the other? For centuries dogs have been carefully weeded and tended and trained; with cats, do we not begin afresh with each generation, instead of guarding the race with care and strengthening by selection their good points.

Rosa Barret, *The Times*, 29 June 1895

Bibliography

Newspapers and Magazines
Country Times
Dundee Advertiser
Durham Advertiser
Gentleman's Magazine, The
Glasgow Herald
Illustrated London News
Land and Water
London Gazette
Manchester Guardian
Newcastle Chronicle
Newcastle Journal
Observer, The
Rambler, The
Spectator, The
Time and Tide
Times, The

Books
Austen, Adelaide, *A Book of Favourite Animals, Domestic and Wild*, 1871
Batty, Beatrice, *Mätzchen and His Mistresses: A True Story*, 1881
Carrington, Edith, *True Stories about Animals*, 1904

Chappell, Jennie, *Animals Worth Knowing: True Stories of the Intelligence of Animals and Birds*, 1911

Clan of the Cats: True Stories about the Feline Animals, 1877

Domestic Animals, 1888

Gask, L., *Not Worth His Salt*, 1910

Gray: Poetry & Prose, 1926

Hall, S. C., and Harrison Weir, *Animal Sagacity*, 1866

Jackman, Francis, *Journeyman*, 1867

Jensen, Peter, *High Days and Holidays*, 1922

Loudon, *Domestic Pets: Their Habits and Management*, 1851

Our Dumb Animals, 1930

Seymour, Daphne, *Kin and Kind*, 1870

Smith, J.B.H., *Memories*, 1913

Southey, Robert, *The Poetical Works of Robert Southey*, 1899

Strachey, John St. Loe, *Cat and Bird Stories from the Spectator*, 1896

True Stories about Animals, 1858

Tyrrell, W. H., *Animal Sagacity*, 1819

Wood, J. G., *Our Domestic Pets*, 1870